Plants & Flowers
in the Home

Plants & Flowers
in the Home

Violet Stevenson

LONGMEADOW
PRESS

Contents

First published in the USA by
Longmeadow Press, PO Box 16,
Rowayton Station, Norwalk,
Connecticut 06853

© 1975 Hennerwood
Publications Limited

ISBN 0 904230 12 0

Produced by Mandarin
Publishers Limited
Hong Kong

Printed in Hong Kong

Introduction

Decoration with growing plants has always been popular and although we sometimes read of 'contemporary' plants, the pot plant in the home is no recent introduction. It is the way that plants are used that has changed so tremendously during the past two decades. A plant is no longer an afterthought. It is an embellishment, an applied decoration, lasting longer than fresh cut flowers and in so many senses, serving a fuller purpose. Plants are a necessity. They add to our happiness and our tranquillity. They are living things and so easy to live with.

Where at one time plants seemed to stand isolated in a home, usually on a sill or in a window, having no real share in the homely things around them, they now play an important decorative role. In this book we shall see how plants can be used both with and in lieu of furnishings. We shall see how to draw them into the general theme of home decoration. How to place them, how to use them to advantage in more ways than one, how to mix them and arrange them and, of course, how to buy, grow and care for them.

Most people begin by buying their plants. Some continue to do so but there are others who discover that they would like to raise some plants of their own. This subject will also be discussed—fortunately, so many house plants can be raised easily from cuttings.

Not all house plants bloom and not all of those which do have conspicuous or even beautiful flowers, at least not when seen with the naked eye. However most people want flowers as well as leaves around them. So after describing the house plants we can grow well, we shall go on to discuss how fresh flowers can be arranged and used to the greatest advantage. And from the display of fresh flowers, whose lives alas are so fleeting, it is a short, logical step to arranging dried flowers.

These, like today's plants, also play a new role. With plants, dried flowers share the estimable quality of remaining lovely for long periods in warm interiors—in rooms which often are responsible for cut flowers maturing and so fading, too quickly. Central heating calls for its own kind of decoration!

Dried flowers can look as attractive as any other kind. Gone is the Victorian dust-trapping birds' nest type of bouquet of immortelles and grasses and in its place we can have both modern and classically styled flower arrangements, montage and all kinds of decorative designs, if these are required. In these, the old favourite flowers are combined with a wealth of new 'perpetuelles' now drawn from all parts of the globe and on sale everywhere. Dried flowers are delightful complements to green, living plants and they can stand between a plant and some source of dry heat, an attractive but effective barrier, protecting the plant in a convenient manner since so many plants need a humid atmosphere.

Once you have arranged flowers many times it will become natural to think also of arranging plants. These can be treated in much the same way as flowers and grouped together still in their pots in temporary arrangements or else given a more permanent value and beauty by transplanting them and mixing them in a larger container.

Once you have seen how attractive such arrangements can be you will not hesitate to take that short step to making pot-et-fleur, mixing plants and cut flowers. Indeed you might begin unprompted simply by enlivening a bowl of plants which look past their best. You will soon appreciate that this is another fascinating form of flower arrangement in its widest sense.

Throughout this book are examples of many ways in which all these subjects have been and can be used. While it is hoped that the reader will find them attractive and appealing enough to want to copy them, it is also hoped that this book will become an inspiration to all who love plants and who would like to arrange them instead in his or her own special individual way. Through it we hope to promote a much wider use of plants and flowers in the home.

House Plants

Understanding plants

ur plants are to remain decorative for as long as ible we have to get to know and understand them. t of all we should realise that a house plant is not ly any different from a garden or wild plant except s much as we have brought it into the home. It is ial because it is attractive and adaptable. A house t is one that is grown indoors under normal living ditions.

et often our living conditions are not those of the t if it were growing naturally. House plants have me such because of their adaptability – we really ld call them home plants. How marvellous it is a plant which comes from the dim, steamy jungle, live cosily inside four walls in different climate and and that next to it a cactus from the hot, arid

desert will bloom on a sunny kitchen windowsill.

Indoor plants vary just as much as those which grow out of doors for there are herbaceous kinds, shrubs, trees, climbers and creepers, bulbs, tubers, corms and rhizomes. There are perennials, biennials and annuals. There are evergreen and deciduous plants. There are those we prize for their foliage and others which we admire for their flowers. There are even some indoor plants we grow for their fruits. There are plants to suit us all and the different ways in which we live.

For the sake of convenience house plants are divided into two groups, temporary and permanent plants. The terms speak for themselves although one should realise that permanent needs to be taken at its hairdresser's value. Generally speaking, the temporary plants may be considered to have a life, once brought into the home, which is measured in weeks while that of the permanent plants may be measured in months or even years. We should aim for years. Fortunately many are both agreeable and adaptable.

The temporary plants are more familiar to more people than the permanent kinds. They include such flowering kinds as azaleas, cyclamen, heaths, primulas, cinerarias, the berried solanums and capsicums and the ornamental leaved coleus, the scented exacum and crassulas. All of which have been grown with one aim; that they should be at their best when they reach the customer. It is only natural that one should want the flowers to go on as long as possible. Yet what so often happens is that from the moment the plant is brought into the home its flowers slowly but steadily decline in beauty and life. This need not happen. If we can learn

Previous page
Solanum capsicastrum. Unless it is in cool surroundings this little plant cannot be expected to live for long in the home. Water it carefully, spray the entire plant with clean tepid water daily and keep it as far as possible from any source of heat.

Left
Bromeliads. Two species of the bromeliad cryptanthus. The tallest is *C. bromelioides* 'Tricolor' of which the young growth is often rose-tinted, the other, *C. fosterianus* is distinguished by its across-the-leaf markings. These are excellent plants as they thrive in most normal home conditions.

Below
Aechmea rhodocyanea. This is one of the easiest of all house plants to grow, and to water, simply keep the centre vase always full. The inflorescence is both brilliantly coloured and long-lasting. It may be increased by offsets such as can be seen low left.

Right
Many new species of cacti are constantly being introduced, and those already familiar to cacti-lovers have become great favourites. *Parodia microsperma* shown here comes from Argentina, and is a member of a large family of cacti many of which are easy to cultivate.

Below
Cryptanthus zonatus. This is an agreeable cryptanthus (known as the Zebra plant) which lends itself to all kinds of decorative schemes. It can be grown in a pot, in mixed arrangements, used in pot-et-fleur or even fixed with other small bromeliads to a mossed branch. The leaves can grow up to 9 inches in length.

to appreciate the plant's needs we ought to be ab enjoy it to the full. Fortunately, it does not take lor get to know plants.

The four things that plants get in their early days help them to grow and give them a good start in life warmth, light and humidity, steady temperature freedom from draughts. Of these basic requirements healthy plant, we are normally able to supply warmth and light. For in our homes temperatures to fluctuate, usually they rise to a peak in the eve and then swiftly drop during the night. We may p ourselves on the air in our rooms being nice and dry our plants need humidity. It is really surprising v plants will put up with. It is also surprising how ea is to give them what they need. It so happens, as shall see, that in making a plant comfortable, in suring that it shall live as long as possible, we also n it more decorative. It settles in more attractively becomes part of the environment.

As you would expect, those plants which are r popular, most often seen, are the toughest. The s goes for those which have been around for a long such as aspidistras, palms of many kinds, rubber pl and ivies. If you see the same kind of plant growing under many different conditions it follows that th an easy type and if you are new to house plants would do well to get one like it.

Indoor plants are rather like pets. They have diffe habits, different needs, according to their kind. will get to know a plant as you would get to know a For instance, one kind of plant may need watering

e sansevieria, tough and
aptable, will live for years. It
ighly decorative and
vides splendid contrasts of
our, texture and shape to
ups and arrangements,
nonstrated here in a group
ich includes a scindapsus,
argonium crispum and
eromias.

once a week, but should it stand in a very sunny, well ventilated yet warm room, it may sometimes need watering every day. It is important for the new indoor gardener to realize that he or she is very much in command. Mostly, someone who cannot see either the plant or its setting can do no more than generalize.

Fortunately, there are a few plants which are so tough, so house or home-hardy, that it is possible to give fairly precise directions for certain aspects of their care. These ensure that the plants live. Whether they thrive, flourish and even flower is in the hands of the plant owner.

Among these easy-going types are some in a family known as bromeliads. The pineapple is a typical, though tall, member and because a bromeliad other plants belonging to this family are known as room pines. While it is possible to grow an ordinary pineapple indoors and even to have it bear fruit, it is the lovely variegated forms which are most often seen.

Possibly the best known of the family is *Aechmea fasciata* the Greek vase or urn plant. The vernacular name comes from the shape of the plant, the bases of its leaves overlap and form a vase in which water will remain. This reservoir is a characteristic of bromeliads. Some have a more pronounced vessel than others but it is effective all the same. In the wild state and growing on trees, the plants trap their water this way. In the home, where they are mostly grown in pots of soil they can still take their water this way though it is also possible to grow them on wood. It is comforting to know that all you have to do is to keep the centres filled with water.

There are several species and varieties of bromeliads on sale and it is possible gradually to make a collection. Cryptanthus species are flatter and more star-like than the tall aechmeas. Vriesia and neoregelia come between the two. All have strange, handsome markings and some are vividly coloured with brilliant reds and coral pinks. They produce odd, and tiny or conspicuous and strangely beautiful flowers. They look so wonderfully exotic that it is hard to believe that they really are easy—but they are. They live for years and after flowering they send up new shoots or offsets from which you can propagate more plants. They will grow in many places in a home, from a fireplace to a sunny window. Some of them are delightful subjects in mixed arrangements of plants or plants and flowers which are known as pot-et-fleur.

Resembling the taller bromeliads in some ways with its long pointed leaves and handsome leaf markings, the sansevieria, a member of the lily family, shares their agreeable toughness and adaptability. It too will live for years and will grow so large in time, widthways not in height, that you can either divide it into several smaller plants or repot it into containers of ever-increasing girth and so allow both it and your reputation as an indoor gardener to grow to a great size.

Its right to be included in the easy plant group is due to the fact that you can water it in the same way as you water cacti, once a month from October to March and then once a week. During summer a little soluble plant food will be welcome.

The sansevierias have thick chunky leaves. They are semi- or sub-succulent and as such are able to store water. This is the reason why they can be left unwatered for so long. Too much water poured into the pot soil will cause the leaves to rot at their bases.

They also are plants which will grow almost anywhere, even tolerating low temperatures from time to time. They tend to remain static where conditions are not really to their liking and often you will find that if a plant is moved to some more agreeable situation it

Right
Rebutia kupperiana. Many of the species are easily raised from seed. Not only do the plants themselves produce this freely but it germinates quickly. Sometimes you will find seedlings growing round the parent plant. The flowers remain for about a week and close at night.

Below left
Vriesia splendens and *Aloe aristata.* Many plants grown for the beauty, shape and texture of their foliage also produce attractive flowers. Here, the spikey inflorescence of the vriesia is seen contrasting with the pendent flowers of the aloe. Vriesias are bromeliads, and aloes are leaf succulents which often produce growth in winter and should also produce frequent offsets.

Below right
Epiphyllum ackermannii. This particular plant which itself produces gorgeous showy flowers is the parent of many other handsome hybrids. These have a delightful colour range and beautiful blooms. See also pages 19 and 48.

Far right
Chamaecereus silvestrii is known also as the pea-nut cactus and the prostrate cereus. It is usually happy in a sunny position where it will produce two-inch-long flowers from May to July.

will produce several new shoots quite quickly. If this happens, take the hint and let it remain in its new home. Because of their tall, spiky outlines, sansevierias look well in arrangements.

Another member of the same family, *Aloe variegata*, sometimes called the partridge plant because of its bird-like bars and dots, is also easy. It is often to be seen in windows and although it will grow in sunshine it will also flourish in a shady window, if this is not a contradiction in terms. This aloe also is succulent.

This term – succulent – is used to describe a plant and it is also the term for particular types of plants. Cacti are succulent by nature and also botanically. These are very easy plants to grow and once you have coaxed a cactus into flower it will continue to bloom each year. Some have some very gorgeous blooms, others are small and even dowdy but what they lack in flower power they tend to make up for in plant form and texture. Cacti do not produce leaves. They have plant bodies. Unless they are very fine specimens, cacti do not create a striking decorative effect if they are just stood about in little pots. On the other hand, they do lend themselves well to all kinds of massing and grouping, as we shall see. They are not suitable for mixing with other plants since their water requirements differ.

There are three distinct tribes of cacti. Those in Tribe 1, the pereskieae, are not usually of interest to the house plant collector. Tribe 2 contains most of those we see on sale and which are so good for grouping and for filling bowls and dish gardens. Tribe 3 contains the cereus or night-blooming cacti. Among the loveliest of all, and certainly the most decorative for indoors, are the epiphytic species known loosely as epiphyllums or leaf-flowering cacti. The latter name is really a mis-nomer because the flowers are not produced on leaves but on flattened stems or plant bodies which somewhat resemble leaves. Most people know the vividly coloured, prettily pendent Christmas cactus, which is just one of the many lovely plants in this group. These can be very decorative and well grown they will make really large plants which become smothered with dozens of blooms.

Often cacti and succulents, from several different plant families, are grouped together under the 'Cactus' heading. It is important to understand that not all succulents are cacti.

One non-cactus family, crassulaceae, contains so many lovely succulent plants which are a delight to the

indoor gardener. Their great appeal is that they are beautiful, even when not in bloom. Unlike most cacti, they have no spines. Their leaves are thick, chunky, sometimes wavy-edged, prettily shaped and sometimes gorgeously coloured or perhaps covered with a blue-grey bloom like a grape. Individual plants are often flower-like in form, reminding one of great, thick-petalled roses. Often they are sessile (stemless) and their great rosettes spread out over the soil and out beyond the pot rim. Others in this family carry their plant rosettes on thick, stout trunks and sometimes there will be several rosettes to one stalk. *Aeonium tabulae-forme* is a handsome example. This, like so many in this family, is a good plant for the beginner who will be enchanted with the long well branching flower stem which supports a mass of dainty primrose-coloured flowers.

Many of these succulents produce spectacular flowers, the coral coloured echeveria and the bell-shaped oliveranthus, really an echeveria, are examples. Among this group are the dainty species of crassulas and the fragrant rochea. Some of these closely resemble a kalanchoes and you are likely to find them in bowls of mixed plants which have been assembled and marketed by the florist or nurseryman.

So long as all of these are kept in a temperature of round about 10°C. or 50°F., they will prove to be both easy and rewarding. If you are short of house room they, like cacti, can be stood outdoors for the summer.

Even with the few types we have already discussed, the bromeliads, the lily family succulents, cacti and the crassulas, we have the beginnings of an attractive collection in which there are contrasts of shape, texture, colour and size.

A group of plants which have been standing around indoors, in many countries, for a very long time are the so-called potted palms. These really are tolerant. They will flourish under the most difficult conditions, or so it seems. They must surely be the most undemanding of all of the plants we grow. The palms you are most likely to find on sale are the *Chamaedorea elegans*, a graceful, slow-growing little beauty which is just the right size for many arrangements although it looks very well on its

Right
Unlike most other cacti that can be grown at home, *Aporocactus flagelliformis* has drooping stems, sometimes as long as two feet. As a result it is known as the Rat's tail cactus and it looks well placed on a pedestal or in a hanging basket.

Far right
Rhipsalidopsis gaertneri syn. *Schlumbergera gaertneri*. Revelling in good light, this particular leaf-flowering cactus blooms in spring, hence its popular name, the Easter cactus.

own, especially if it can be silhouetted in some way—this goes for all palms; you may find this on sale under its synonyms, *Neanthe elegans* or *N. bella* and *Collinia elegans*; *Phoenix dactylifers*, the date palm, sometimes sold as cocos (which it is not, that name belongs to the coconut palm) and perhaps other phoenix species such as *P. roebelinii* and *P. canariensis*, *Butis capitata* whose synonym is *Cocos capitata*; *Howea belmoreana* (synonym *Kentia belmoreana*) the curly palm and *H. fosteriana*, *(K. fosteriana)* the flat or thatch leaf palm, and *Livistone chinensis*, the Chinese fan palm.

So often, when one buys a palm, it seems much too large for its pot and one's first impulse is to repot it to give its roots more living room. However, this would be a mistake, for palms appear to grow best where their roots are restricted. It is possible to keep a plant for as long as two or three years in a 60 pot (3 inch), but plants in such small pots are difficult to deal with and become top heavy. As a temporary expedient plants in too small a pot may be placed, small pot included, in a larger and heavier pot. Pot-bound plants, the term for those whose roots really fill the pots, will require more frequent watering than those which have plenty of soil between their roots which hold more water. For this reason palms and many other plants, as we shall learn, are best plunged, but more of that later.

Palms were at the height of their popularity during the last century during which time two other deep green plants were also much sought after and cherished. One of these was the aspidistra, now rare enough in some countries to be a collector's item. Known then as the

parlour plant and as the cast iron plant it flourished dim, smoky rooms as well as well-lit surroundings. summer it was stood outdoors so that its leaves co become cleansed by the summer rains and in win it went back to its place not so very far from the coal f It is a plant which is most difficult to kill. It will se up new leaves in spite of bad treatment, yet if you w to treat it as lovingly as the most precious new plan your care you would find that it is the ugly duckl among house plants. Grown in good compost, repot from time to time, given regular watering and feedi it gradually turns into a lovely green swan! A go specimen is among the most handsome of all ho plants. It will grow high, wide and handsome. A go plant could fill a wide fireplace.

There is a variegated form, *A. elatior* 'Variega which, though not quite so robust as the green type very attractive. If you find one, keep it in a sligh warmer temperature and in stronger light than green species but keep it out of direct sunlight.

Probably one of the best known of all our ho plants is the so-called rubber plant, *Ficus elast* 'Decora', yet it too was a favourite Victorian 'gre In its natural state this ficus becomes a very tall bran ing tree but the potted plants are usually grown sin stemmed. The plant grows slowly, a quality, really some house plants for once they are in place in the h it is usually most convenient to have them stay in same position. A good plant should be well clothed w leaves right down to the base of its stem.

It is a jungle plant which means that it can tolera

Below
Those who enjoy collecting strange plants often keep a *Stapelia variegata* or some other species of this family of strange succulents which produce fantastic and enormous blooms. Unfortunately some of these have a carrion odour and so the plants cannot always be kept in a much used room.

Far right
Epiphyllum hybrid. One of the many lovely epiphyllums which can be grown indoors. Their colour range is good, from near white through yellow, orange, red, crimson and rose. Their usual height is one to two feet and there are no true leaves—the stems are flattened and look like thick leaves.

good deal of shade, its dark leathery leaves are an indication of this. Plants grown back in a room have better looking foliage than those which are grown in a sunny place.

There are other species and varieties of ficus which make good house plants although most of them differ in appearance from the rubber plant. Some, like *F. pumila*, are trailers which will cling to a wall if they get the chance and if conditions are right. For instance, if you wished to clothe a wall, stand or plant this ficus near it and keep the wall surface sprayed from time to time. Other ficus have smaller leaves and are more branching in habit than *F. elastica*. *F. benjamina* much resembles a neat citrus tree except, of course, that it does not bear coloured fruits. Mature plants of some of the ficus species do produce little green fruits and you may find them familiar in appearance because ficus is the fig genus or family.

A tall fig is extremely striking in appearance and well deserves the term architectural which is often applied to it. This term is also sometimes used to describe another jungle plant with tough, leathery, deep green leaves, the monstera. While the figs' leaves are simple, those of the monstera are irregular in outline with great slashes and even holes through the leaves. The latter have caused it to be known to some people as the Gruyere cheese plant.

So long as one observes a few simple rules, this handsome plant is easy to grow. It likes a shady position and

vea belmoreana (syn.
ia). Palms are both
orative and very long-lived.
y appear to grow best when
r roots are restricted and
hey should not be repotted
uently. However, pot
nd palms need more water
those which still have
ty of soil between their
s.

ve
s benjamina is just the
t for those who admire the
ities of *F. elastica* (see
wing page) but not its
or form. Neat, evergreen
prettily branching, it is
iest in rooms where the
erature is never below
(10°C).

t
indomitable aspidistra,
so common, is now a
y in some countries. It
struggle to live in bad
itions, but fed and well
for it will make a
some and decorative

it likes to be left to grow in the one place. It likes plenty of pot room and you can always tell when it should be repotted because the leaves become less and less slashed and holed. It is a plant for spacious interiors or for some place where it can roam a wall.

The monstera is botanically allied to philodendron and, as we shall see, there are very many of the arcid family (the Araceae) that make attractive house plants, especially those which like the monstera are climbers. The arum lily is probably the most easily recognised of these. There are several good house plants in this group but not all of them are easy. Many of them flower and some, like the spathiphyllum have white arum-like blooms. Others have green 'arums'. One of the easy and agreeable species is *Syngonium podophyllum* which continues to flourish even under what might be considered to be poor conditions. Like many philodendrons it can be persuaded to grow in water or in sand and water or pebbles and water. As one can appreciate, this facility opens the way to different methods of displaying plants, think for instance of the variety of vessels which can then become plant containers. This method of growing will be discussed more fully later on.

Like the bromeliads and the epiphyllums already discussed, philodendrons are also tree growing—epiphytes. Often a new indoor gardener is puzzled by the strange thong-like growths which appear on the stems of some of these plants. These are aerial roots through which the plant takes in moisture from the air, its other kind of roots are used in anchoring it to the ground and clinging to the tree on which it grows. When they appear on house plants these roots are best trained down into the soil of the pot.

Of all the philodendrons, *P. scandens*, with deep green heart shaped leaves (because of these it is sometimes called sweetheart plant), is possibly the easiest of all to grow. It is also tolerant and can be moved around more than most. Although a climber when given support, it is also a pretty trailer and so is useful in plant arrangements.

Equally tough, in my experience, is a species with much larger leaves, *P. erubescens*, of which there is a form with coppery young leaves known as 'Burgundy'. It is a climber but it grows very slowly and what might appear to be a bushy plant when bought might stay that way for a very long time and then gradually begin to extend its stem and climb.

Also tough is *P. bipinnatifidum*, a non-climbing plant with large feathered leaves of deep, glossy green. These three and others which are on sale, can be grown well back in a room if required.

Where house plants are grown for their decorative qualities, climbing kinds are an essential. Monsteras and certain philodendrons will play this role but there are a few other tough and agreeable plants which also should be considered. Among these are two close relatives to the grape vine, *Cissus antarctica*, which has simple tooth-edged leaves and *Rhoicissus rhomboidea*, which has prettily divided leaves. We shall be meeting these two again.

As one would expect, climbers which also trail are useful to the decorator and if they are also varied in colouration with many hues of green, with white, grey and yellows, they become even more so. The ubiquitous ivies are such plants. The simple, small-leaved green species *Hedera helix* has been a treasured house plant for a long time and it has repaid our love and interest by sporting and producing a remarkable range of different ivies which for convenience sake are known as varieties. So far as easy plants are concerned, here again the old rule proves sound, that the greener the leaf the more tolerant the plant. However, leaf texture also

Above left
Philodendron scandens and *Scindapsus aureus*. Of all the philodendrons, *P. scandens* i possibly the easiest to grow. It trails as prettily as it climb The same can be said of scindapsus, although it is a more tender plant which doe not tolerate direct sunshine and needs to be kept moist.

Right
Monstera deliciosa in the foreground with a howea by the windows. A large specim like this will grow in a comparatively small pot for three or four years before needing repotting. When mature, it will produce creamy-coloured spikes whi are followed by cone-shapec edible fruits.

Left
Known popularly as the rubber plant, *Ficus elastica* has been a valued house pla for many decades. 'Decora' an improved cultivar of the original and there are other varieties to be found as well *F. elastica* can easily grow u to ten feet in a tub if you allow it to.

Following page
Philodendron bipinnatifidu This particular plant has l for five years in a room wh it receives no direct light. you can see, its leaves turn towards the main light sou Philodendrons generally a tolerant plants. Keep then warm, fairly humid, but never in bright sunshine.

seems to be of some influence so far as the ivy is concerned and those varieties such as *H. h.* 'Glacier', with small leaves charmingly coloured in grey and white, which have tough textured leaves, as opposed to silky, will tolerate the same dim or away-from-light situations as *H. helix*. On the other hand, large silky-leaved plants such as the cream and green *H. canariensis*, another species altogether, needs a different situation, in good light but not in direct sunlight.

Anyone who hopes to make many plant arrangements throughout the year would do well to build up a stock of varied ivies. These are both cheap to buy and easy to propagate. No other plant, except perhaps the pretty little tradescantia, scrambles so attractively over the edge of a bowl or some other container.

If ivies are given support they will climb. They will also cling, to ceiling or wall should you wish them to do so. If the plants are grown in a tall container or raised from the floor level by some other means, they will also send some of their trails down over the rim and so furnish the lower levels of the plant easily and attractively.

As you can see from these few descriptions, house plants vary considerably. As a general rule, the more highly coloured the foliage the more difficult the plant. For example, crotons are perhaps the most gorgeous of all house plants but unless they are grown inside a Wardian glass case or some other enclosed container, a carboy for instance, these will not last for long. Some of the dracaenas have lovely colouration and these also are a little on the temperamental side. Often such plants will grow quite well during the summer months and it is a good plan to introduce them into the home at that time so that they can gradually adapt themselves to their surroundings.

On the other hand, there are some almost hardy garden plants which make good house plants. These could be so useful for those who want some plants for a situation in which it is not possible to provide much warmth, an outer landing to a flat for instance. Ivies, which might take a few weeks to become adjusted if they have been brought from a warm greenhouse, *Araucaria excelsa* or Norfolk Island Pine, fatsia and fatshedera and forms of euonymus are examples.

Far right
Cissus antarctica, popular called the kangaroo vine, be grown as a pillar or w its long trails divided to c wall. As its specific name indicates, it prefers a coo situation to one which is warm and arid.

Right and Below right
Rhoicissus rhomboidea (th grape ivy) will fit into ma places in the home. Here climbing well and being encouraged to frame an archway leading from kit to dining room. If require it can be kept neat and b by pinching out the tips c growing stems. It looks attractive placed at the e of a group or arrangemen that some of its trails can cascade prettily, and will well away from direct lig

Flowering plants

Most flowering plants have to be regarded as temporary decorations. Fortunately, they are so extremely beautiful that what they lack in staying power they make up for in colour and general beauty. It is quite natural that most of us should wish to keep them for as long as possible, perhaps to bloom another year, but this is seldom possible.

So many of our flowering plants are annuals, examples are cineraria, exacum, browallia, and once these have flowered they die. There are some flowering kinds which are perennials treated as annuals, which means that they can be brought quickly into bloom but this causes them to expend their energies so freely that they are soon spent once they have flowered.

Other perennials and some shrubs, azaleas and

Left
A November display of cyclamen, begonias and cinerarias. All these plants need careful watering if they are to live any length of time.

Below
Anthurium scherzerianum. Known as the Piggy-tail plant, because of their curly spadices, these anthuriums are really quite tough house plants. They grow best in good light, without this they will not flower. They dislike draughts and dry conditions.

Right
Caladium with Hippeastrum, which is popularly though wrongly called amaryllis, has such spectacular flowers that it is hard to believe that the bulbs are easily grown. It is sometimes possible to buy prepared, ready-potted bulbs which will flower very quickly. Plant the bulbs singly in a loam based compost leaving the top of the bulb exposed and keep moist until the leaves die down.

Opposite page top
A west-facing window is an ideal spot in which to grow an assortment of plants. Among these flowering here are an epiphyllum hybrid, an Easter cactus and the dark-leaved *Impatiens wellariana petersiana*. Impatiens are shrubby semi-succulent plants which have clusters of bright flowers. Some of them are perennials and tip cuttings can be taken at any time.

Below right
Hyacinths will grow in water alone with a nugget of charcoal put at the bottom to keep the water sweet. There are special glasses made to hold the bulbs. A little grass sprinkled over the soil surface furnishes a simple flower pot. Crocuses, scillas and most small-flowering bulbs should not be brought indoors until the buds are ready to open.

Below far right
Many lilies can be grown quite well in pots of soil like any other bulbs. There are some, like this midcentury hybrid, 'Enchantment' which are sold ready potted and prepared to flower quickly with the minimum of attention.

heaths (*Erica*), are subjected to even more severe methods of cultivation and by various means are forced into bloom completely out of their natural season. It is not the purpose of this book to explain these processes but it is important that I should point out that should such a plant continue to live after it has finished flowering it is most unlikely to produce flowers again in the following year in the same season. Usually, such plants take two or three years to become adjusted. Poinsettias are the best known examples.

On the other hand there are many other much more permanent plants which flower prettily and for more than one year at a time. Some, like saintpaulia or African violets may flower more than once a year.

Some of these may be grown for their flowers alone, their leaves being unremarkable and the plants themselves not highly decorative except when in bloom. There are also many foliage plants which reward one with the odd flower or two. As I described earlier, aechmeas and some other bromeliads produce unusual flowers which are extremely decorative and long lasting, others are more interesting than decorative. The same applies to aroids, anthurium and spathiphyllum produce showy blooms but others may be green and leaf-like.

Lovely flowering plants which present few problems are those which are grown from bulbs. These can be bought in pots and bowls already planted and in bud or bloom. Alternatively, the indoor gardener can grow them from the very beginning. The bulb is planted in bulb fibre, soil, water or water and pebbles – according to its kind. If the bulb has to be forced into flower out of season, it is usually expendable for it will not flower in the same way nor at the same time the following year. Often forced bulbs of hardy plants, hyacinths, tulips and daffodils, for instance, can be planted in the garden and there they will gradually recuperate and bloom again one day.

Some bulbous plants are perennial indoors in the sense that they can be saved and grown again year after year. Often these have to be rested which means that they remain in their pots but are not watered. When the time comes they are repotted, watered and started into growth again. Hippeastrums, sometimes called amaryllis, hymenocallis, sprekelia, lapeyrousia and nerines are examples and all of these can be bought easily from bulb merchants.

More and more kinds of bulbs are being marketed ready planted but not grown. These bulbs have also

29

been specially prepared and their cultivation is simplicity itself. The gardener is so well rewarded for the minimum of effort, one simply follows the bulb merchant's instructions. Often there is nothing to do but to water the pot and stand it in good light and soon there are gorgeous hippeastrums, lilies, lilies-of-the-valley, tulips, narcissi, hyacinths or colchicums to admire. All is astonishingly easy. New types of bulbs which can be grown this way are being introduced annually. It is also possible to buy prepared bulbs of certain kinds of flowers and to plant these yourself.

Whatever group flowering plants might fall into generally speaking there are a few rules which apply to all. Except for a very few kinds, spathiphyllum, a shade lover is an example, plants in bloom need good light though not, as has been stressed already, direct sunlight which might scorch them.

If the plant is not highly decorative when not in flower, you might find it convenient to move it around and to keep it in some less obvious place until its flower buds show. However, do choose the new site with care.

You can tell if a plant is not getting enough light because its stems become drawn and floppy and its flowers are not as well coloured as they should be. We shall discuss the influence of light on plants more fully later. Obviously, if you notice signs you should take action. Conversely, if you notice the blooms on a plant have suddenly flopped, even petals clinging together instead of being wide apart, you should move the plant to a less sunny place, for the time being at least. If you have no other site but a sunny windowsill, hang a fine curtain between the glass and the plant.

However, it may not be light alone which is causing the trouble. Water and humidity are also essential to flowering plants and at times, lack of these two may be critical.

One group of flowering plants which seems to do best in a really sunny window and in a dry atmosphere is the pelargonium, popularly called geranium. Although they are more often grown outdoors in windowboxes and hanging baskets than in the home, they are in fact good decorative house plants. They must have good light. Sometimes in summer a plant in a very hot and sunny situation will loose too much water and droop its leaves and should this happen it should either be given a larger pot or moved to some other place. The plants produce flowers intermittently throughout winter, even those which have been grown outdoors and are

This page
The commercial grower can induce chrysanthemums to flower all year round. He can also dwarf them to make compact and floriferous pot plants. Like most flowering plants, and the berried solanums with them here, they need good light.

Right
Some of the most popular gift plants. Of these the azalea and heaths should be kept constantly moist at the roots. Primulas and chrysanthemums need cool situations if they are to last well. *Solanum capsicastrum* and a prettily variegated ivy complete the picture.

brought in for decoration during the winter months.

Azaleas and heathers should never be allowed to dry out and are always best plunged. Feed these fortnightly when they are in bud and water them with rain water.

Cinerarias are among the very few plants which do best if they are watered every day. Certainly, they should never be allowed to become dry at the roots for once these plants wilt they will never properly revive.

Becoming almost dry at the roots does not harm some plants as much as one might expect. Indeed, the aeration caused by the rushing of the water through the dry soil and out through the pot is beneficial to the roots, but this does not apply to many flowering kinds.

Other plants which, like cinerarias need watering and feeding liberally are calceolarias. These need a warmer temperature than the foregoing but like them they need really good light.

The many little pot chrysanthemums now on sale, usually dwarf and very compact and grown under intense scientific cultivation, are often found to have small pots packed full of roots. This being the case, the plants need plenty of water. In a warm room, perhaps

...mulas are attractive ...ering plants and there are ...mber of different species; ...large-flowered *Primula* ...*nica* and the daintier ...*alacoides* are probably ...best known. They like ...ty of water and light ...ing when in flower. Plants ...be raised from seed quite ...y. Also in the picture is a ...dard azalea, a sansevieria ...a small-leaved ivy.

...right

...dly coloured cinerarias ...calceolarias will last ...er and produce more ...ms if they are watered ...ally and fed whilst in ...er. There are many lovely ...ties of both kinds of ...ts in a gorgeous range of ...urs.

...t

...rangeas are an exception ...e general rule and are ...ng the few flowering ...se plants which do best ...me shade. If they are ...d in full sunlight they are ...y to flag too badly ever ...e fully revived to their ...er brilliance.

Right
Hoya carnosa. There is also
a charming variegated variety
of this plant as well as the
green-leaved *H. bella* which
produces even more brilliant
wax-flowers, as they are called.
A climber, the hoya is a little
slow in beginning, but speedy
once established.

Opposite above
A group of three flowering
plants showing greatly differing
'blooms'. The 'rat tails' are
the flowers of *Peperomia
glabella*, on the left are the red
piggy tails of an anthurium,
and behind are the vivid blue
flowers of browallia, which is
an annual and easily raised
from seed. Peperomias like a
humid atmosphere and the pot
soil should be kept fairly dry
in winter.

Opposite below
Some ornamental-leaved
begonias flower prettily, like
this *Begonia haageana*. There
are many species and varieties
which will grow well, even
luxuriantly, indoors so long as
they have warmth and some
humidity.

daily. If there are still many buds to open it is also wise to feed them weekly because the plant foods become leached out by so much water.

Hydrangeas need much the same treatment. These are among the few flowering plants which do best away from strong light.

Solanum capsicastrum the winter cherry and the kinds of pot peppers, capsicum, need very careful watering if they are not to drop their buds and leaves. These grow best when they also can be sprayed daily. Like cyclamen, they prefer a cool atmosphere and good light. While they are in bud, bloom and fruit, they should be fed weekly.

Cyclamen should be watered from the base—the water should be poured into the saucer or whatever other vessel the pot stands in. Better still, they should be plunged. Always avoid pouring water over the corm because droplets tend to rest between the bases of the stems and these cause the corm to rot. One great cause of cyclamen dying apart from incorrect watering are fumes of gas, oil, smoke, paint and others in the atmosphere. Keep them cool, never in a warm room.

Many plants appreciate a little moisture sprinkled or sprayed over their foliage and this is best done in the early morning but not when the sun is shining on the leaves. The reason for this being that droplets can act like a magnifying glass and can burn a leaf.

Primula obconica and *P. sinensis* seem to do best when they are moistened this way and I think that it helps any type of these plants grown indoors, especially any which might be lifted from the garden.

It is not generally known that the garden primroses and polyanthus can be grown in pots on a windowsill in good light. These should be potted in J.I. potting compost in autumn or at any time during winter. If you have no garden, buy garden plants and pot them yourself if they are not being sold already potted.

Most primulas will grow indoors but some are better than others as house plants. *P. kewensis* has fragrant yellow flowers in clusters on tall stems.

Speaking generally, those just mentioned can be grouped as temporary plants and with them the many others that I may not yet have mentioned simply because there is always a continually changing supply of annual flowering plants on the market which may include exacum and browallia, besides some which have vivid foliage such as coleus.

So far as the perennials are concerned, there are people who manage to keep these from one year to the next—an operation which is simplified if one has a greenhouse or conservatory. Azaleas, cyclamen and solanums, for instance, can be kept outdoors, the pots sunk or plunged in garden soil in some partially shaded place. Those who have no gardens sometimes keep the plants on a shady outer windowsill or even indoors in a cool shaded window. At the end of summer the plants are brought indoors or, in the case of those already there, given a little more attention, extra food and water. The azaleas should be repotted in pure peat, well rammed down, after flowering, solanums when they are brought in for the winter and cyclamen corms when they have died down.

Among those flowering plants which are temporary or semi-permanent, according to the skill of the gardeners, are some which are grown from tubers, for example, achimenes, begonias, gloxinias (*sinningia* botanically) and the handsome caladiums which are grown for their colourful leaves and are gorgeous enough to be classed as flowers in this case.

Some begonias do not make tubers and are fibrous-rooted and some of these are also known as winter-flowering begonias.

Many of the flowering plants we shall discuss more fully when we deal with plant arrangements and pot-et-fleur, but just a few words about a special few.

Most columnea species available are beautiful trailing plants with long green-leaved stems which become studded with scarlet-orange flowers.

Euphorbias are varied and the showy poinsettia is one of this family but there are others which resemble cactus plants. Poinsettias are inclined to be temperamental. They dislike too warm rooms, fumes of any sort, draughts either hot or cold and direct sunshine. Their roots should be kept constantly moist and the plant is best plunged. Gardenias, again, are not easy because they need humidity. In some ways it is more important to spray the foliage than to water the soil. Gloxinias, like cyclamen should be watered from below. They need airy not close surroundings but no draughts. *Hoya carnosa*, a pretty little thick-leaved climber is most often sold with its trails trained round in a hoop resting on the rim of the pot. You can unwind these stems and treat the plant like any other climber if you wish but it will go on round and round the hoop if you prefer it that way. This plant must have warmth. Hypocyrta, known as the goldfish plant because of the shape and colour of its little flowers is quite tough and can be grown in a not-so-warm room.

Impatiens or busy lizzie, a great favourite, often appears to thrive in spite of its owners and its surroundings. A well-grown plant should be smothered in flowers. Keep the tips of the shoots pinched out to keep the plant bushy. Feed it when it is in bloom. Keep it warm in winter. Saintpaulia or African violet often fails because of bad light, polluted atmosphere and low temperatures. It grows best when plunged and a bowl or trough of mixed varieties can look very attractive indeed.

Among the bulbous plants you can expect to grow all year round, as opposed to those which have to be planted in the autumn and forced into bloom are the following: clivia with handsome strap-like leaves, haemanthus or blood lily, hippeastrum or amaryllis, hymenocallis, nerine, oxalis, vallota and velthemia.

Below
Euphorbia pulcherrima. Known universally as the poinsettia, this is the most flamboyant member of the spurge family. The vividly coloured bracts surround the tiny berry-like flowers. To keep the colour (red, pink or cream), give the plants plenty of light at all times, but not direct sunlight.

Right
Saintpaulia ionantha 'Diana Blue'. There are many named varieties and some good strains of African violets now available. If you are successful in growing them you will find that they are also easy plants to propagate. They like good light, clean air, humidity and feeding when in flower.

How to choose your plants

Few of us have an opportunity of buying direct from the nursery. Those who live in cities have to buy from a florist or perhaps a garden centre and this means that the plants have left the nursery, travelled to market and been sold there either by the grower's salesman or by a wholesale florist. The retail florist has to buy the plants from the market, transport them to his own establishment and there, finally, place them on show for your selection. Obviously, there have been several opportunities for some harm to come to the plant and with the best will in the world it is not always possible for the retail florist to keep a close enough eye on each of his many plants to ensure that they are always in the best of condition. Furthermore, not all florists are horticulturists and may not recognise that a plant is suffering or is likely to do so.

So far as flowering plants are concerned, our method of marketing means that there is unlikely to be sufficient time for any of the blooms to have passed their peak and be on the way out. Most have some blooms and plenty of buds still to come which is what you should look for. Should you be offered any plant on which it is obvious that even one flower is fading treat it a little suspiciously and select another if you can. Watch out for fading blooms and for those which are flagging or wilting. This may be caused only by thirst and if the plant has been dry only for a short period no harm is done and the situation is soon rectified, but flagging can also be caused through draughts and severe cold. A good guide is to buy plants and flowers rather in the same way as one chooses salad vegetables. Look primarily for crispness and colour. Whether the plant you seek bears flowers or whether it is grown for the beauty of its foliage, a healthy plant has a certain crisp appearance about it. Stems are turgid, stiff, not limp or drooping, even if it should be a trailing kind. Colour should be deep and glowing, leaves should gleam. Be suspicious of any plant which seems faded in appearance. Certain leaves have a metallic sheen on them which is more intensified when they are in the pink of condition. Hairy leaves should look new-brushed and not shabby.

Accept nothing that has spots on it, that is, unnatural spots which are obviously the result of burning or disease. The tissues of these spots will be drier than the main leaf fabric or blistery in appearance. There may be only one spot on a leaf or there may be several. Test the spot by merely wiping the leaf gently between the finger and thumb. Some green plants have a slight deposit caused by the water with which they have been sprayed, particularly if it is limy, but this is easily smoothed away and does no damage.

Some leaves may appear to have a dried brown edging to them. Do not accept a young plant in a small pot in this condition for this is usually an indication of a damaged or sick leaf. However, should the plant be a handsome specimen with very many leaves, begonias

Left
Beloperone guttata. The brownish-rose flowers give this plant its common name of shrimp plant. Although it grows best with some warmth and humidity, cooler and dryer conditions tend to deepen the colour of the attractive bracts. Feed moderately, particularly when in flower.

are examples, it might be that one or two of the older, that is the first formed leaves, are on their way out, as might be expected. They still have a role to play for leaves are the lungs of a plant, its stomach too for that matter, and it is unwise to cut away any leaf while it still has life for it continues to contribute to the well being of the plant and is part of its metabolic system.

A plant should fill its pot. Be suspicious of a plant whose pot looks too large for it. Ailing leaves may have been cut away.

Always examine the growing tips or shoots to make sure that they are sturdy, plump, healthy and capable of further growth. Buds should be succulent. Pointed tips as in philodendrons should be well filled. If they are papery they probably do not contain a living shoot and this indicates that the plant was neglected at some time. There might be future trouble in store. Papery buds do not contain flowers. See that buds are all alike. If you are examining a flowering plant check that there are many more buds to come. If you buy a plant with all its blooms open wide then expect it to be at its best for a short period only.

Whether the plant is a temporary or permanent kind always treat yellowing leaves with suspicion, unless, of course, they are supposed to have some yellow variation in them. Usually, the leaf of a green plant yellows because of ill health and there is a change of texture too. The leaf becomes less tough, sometimes even pappy to the touch. Several yellowing leaves on ivy, cyclamen, from bulbs and others, usually indicate that either the plants are older than they ought to be or very sick, though one leaf may, as has already been suggested, merely be a spent leaf and is no cause for worry.

As I said earlier, a pot should be well filled. Unless stems are naturally leafless, such as those of cyperus which produces little umbrella like topknots, the foliage should always persist to the base. This need not necessarily be thick and bushy but it should be healthy. Plants without tall main stems, such as saintpaulias and begonias should have full crowns. They should fill the pot so well that they cover its rim.

Plants like solanums or winter cherries, heaths and azaleas, all entirely different kinds of plants, show distress by shedding their leaves. One or two only may drop but sometimes these one or two are the beginning of a real fall. If when you are choosing a plant, on the soil surface you see a leaf, or in the case of heaths, some needles do not buy the plant, unless its length of life is really of no consequence. This leaf drop can be caused by more than one factor, drought, draught or insect pests.

So far as size is concerned, all tastes are catered for. Small pots are useful for making plant arrangements and pot-et-fleur. Climbers and plants which are required to stand in a certain place in the home and to act rather as a piece of furniture are best bought in a large pot so that they need never be repotted. The most popular size of pot plant is a 60 or 3 inch, measured across the rim, but there is a large 60 and a small 60. Take care when buying containers that size is taken into account or you will be left with a misfit. It is surprising to discover, as one does, that most 'cover' pots have been designed and made without reference to flower pot sizes. Unless they are arranged and plunged into some moisture retentive medium, small pots are apt to dry out rather quickly once they carry a lot of growth. However, as we shall learn, there are ways of avoiding this. A plant in a 48, the 5 inch pot, is usually about twice the price of the same plant in a 60. Incidentally, pots came by these odd terms because of the way clay pots were made, so many in a cast.

Many flowering plants are sold in 60s and these are

Above right
Calathea zebrina. Closely related to the marantas, calatheas like warmth and humidity. Plants grow best plunged in moist peat inside a larger waterproof pot. They should be kept out of direct sunlight.

Above centre
Crocus chrysanthus 'Princess Beatrix'. All bulbs are safe buys and their successful flowering depends on the conditions and treatment. Crocuses are more difficult than some other bulbs to grow indoors – hyacinths are the easiest for the beginner (see pages 102, 106 for planting instructions).

Far right
Citrus mitis is a rewarding plant to keep at home since it will flower and fruit when young and nearly all the year round. The leathery green leaves quickly indicate if the plant is not healthy by turning yellow.

Right
Gloxinia. With a little planning these flowers can be enjoyed during many months of the year. They can be raised from seed and from cuttings of stem or leaves. The plants form tubers which can be saved from year to year.

40

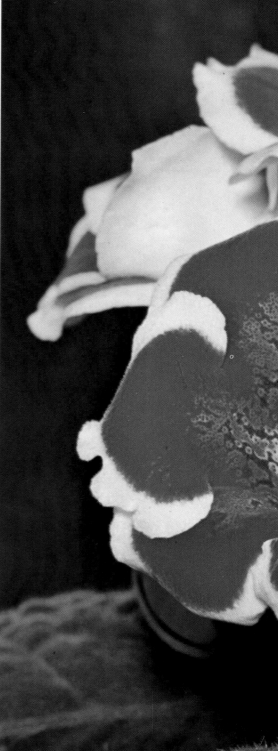

can violets, *Saintpaulia*
ntha, are very varied and
e in colours ranging from
e through pink, rose,
le, violet and blue. These
eautiful flowers from a
hy plant: their colour is
l, there are plenty of buds,
airy leaves and stems are
and well brushed.

dendron scandens and
dendron ilsemanii. The
y pointed tips of
dendron scandens are
filled and the leaves
y and healthy. Leaves of
ants should be kept free
st if they are to remain
hy and attractive.
lar sponging with clean
warm water keeps them

arium fulgens. This is a
l plant to have around
ase it is tolerant and can
oved to fill any odd corner
make a glowing focal
to an arrangement or
o of plants. It is a
eliad and so easy to
—simply keep the central
always filled. The leaves
d be dark and glossy and
grow up to 12 inches long.

Right
Rhododendron simsii. Among the most popular of all flowering house plants, and better known as azaleas, they should be regarded as temporary tenants. More azaleas die of drought than from any other cause, since the root ball must never become dry.

Below
Cyclamen are such popular house plants and there are so many in all florists, particularly around Christmas, that it is important to choose these plants with great care. Check that no leaves show signs of being at all unhealthy and that there are flower buds to come. Many plants are brought on too quickly before they are sold and are consequently difficult to keep.

Far right
Primula obconica is a winter blooming primrose which you can keep from year to year. The colour range is very wide, and again when choosing a plant check that there are plenty of buds to come and that the leaves are a fresh green in colour with their stems firm and upstanding.

Centre right
A really healthy African violet produces flowers which glow strongly with colour.

Below right
Aphelandra squarrosa is a most attractive plant to have in the home. The flowers provide a striking contrast to the dark green banded leaves. Keep the atmosphere moist in summer.

very useful for plant arrangements for they can be treated a little like a bunch of flowers and replaced when they have passed their best.

Azaleas and ericas or heaths are peat-loving and so are potted in peat. This can create problems. If the peat, which is very porous, is allowed to become dry, it shrinks. If the root ball is allowed to remain dry it shrinks and pulls away from the sides of the pot. It is possible to soak the plant and so recharge it but sometimes the drying has gone so far that the re-soaked plant is never the same again. Look at the lower portion of the stalk or little trunk. This should always be moist and darker than the wood above it. When you have the plant at home, keep it this way and then you will know that the roots are moist enough.

If you buy plants for gifts, do not collect them too much in advance of the date when you want to give them. Certainly order these well in advance. If you take the plants home too soon, they will begin to adjust to your own home conditions and then when you pass them on to another home they will have to begin all over again and they may sulk. Your gift will then not be as acceptable as you had hoped.

Never leave plants wrapped. Wrap the plants at the last moment if you must. If you are going by car and the weather is fine you can take plants unwrapped. Otherwise, the best thing is to slip each plant inside a large clear plastic bag so that it is entirely enveloped. Blow into the bag to inflate it so that the plastic stands well away from the leaves and flowers and fasten the top securely. Be generous and use a large bag so that when it is pulled off it does not brush against the plant itself.

Guard against the plant falling over or about. Quite often the best way to secure it is to take a cardboard box, turn it upside down and pierce the centre. From this hole make a few incisions, short or long according to the size of the container and press the pot down into the space thus made open. Allow about two thirds of the pot to go down into the box. The plant will then be elevated and out of harm's way and it will then be possible to push heavy objects against the sides of the box to prevent it moving. Another method, and this is good for small plants, is to fit a box or tray with a block of Oasis foam and to press the pot into this.

If the weather is really cold when you buy plants, avoid street stalls and ignore any plants put on show in the open air. They are likely to succumb later. Always insist on having the whole plant you buy covered and not just the pot. If you can have it slipped into a plastic bag so much the better.

Nurserymen tend to concentrate on those plants which are good do-ers, as you can appreciate. Not only must they grow well but travel well also. A plant must look as well on sale as it did in the nursery. This means that some plants are hard to find, the easy-going plectranthus which is somewhat too brittle to market, is an example. Such plants can often be found at small nurseries, market stalls and horticultural societies' stalls.

Growing hints

Most plants that the nurserymen send out are in soil that will provide sufficient nourishment for plants for a while though it will probably be necessary to feed the plants during their growing season. If a plant fails to thrive one can be almost certain that it is due to the conditions under which it is grown or to the lack of skill on the part of the gardener which are to blame and not the soil in which the plant is growing. Soil mixtures or composts as they are often called are carefully prepared. Mixtures vary sometimes for different plants yet there is a standard soil mixture or compost which suits the majority of plants. It is possible for the indoor gardener to mix his or her own composts and it is possible to buy these from a garden shop or centre.

Many plants die because they have been given too much water and this means that they, or part of them, drown. When there is too much water in the soil, roots die because they cannot breathe. Roots need air as well as moisture. Unless a plant's roots are happy and

growing well it will not be able to function properly above soil level. It is always best to err on keeping a plant a little on the dry side than to allow the soil to remain constantly moist – unless the plant is one which likes a boggy condition, a cyperus is an example.

Roughly speaking, most plants have a root system equal in size to the portion above soil. Of course, in a pot, the roots cannot spread as they would in the open ground. So instead they reach out while the plant is very young and after a time they come to the side of the pot. They then begin to curl around this and in time a plant might form a thick root layer around the sides of a pot. And curiously enough, when a plant has grown in its original pot like this for some time, you will find that there is very little soil left among the roots. When

this happens, the plant needs repotting. Where it i convenient to repot a plant it is possible to ke growing in its crowded container simply by feed regularly with soluble plant food. Usually plan root-bound as this need watering more frequently they would if there was more soil in the pot. If you that a plant is wilting frequently and that you ha give it more and more water, this is most likely to indication that it is root-bound.

As soon as a plant comes into your hands see needs water. There are various tests. One would e it to be enough simply to notice that the soil surf: dry but this could be misleading. The simplest test is to take a scrap of newspaper and with the thumb it on the soil surface. If the soil is moist enoug paper will immediately become damp. Another me is to weigh the pot in your hand. A pot filled with c soil is heavier than one in which there is dry so the pot is made of clay and not plastic you can r with a pencil or some other object. A pot of dry will ring, a pot of moist or wet soil will give a dull sc Once the plant is truly under your care it is likely you will get to know simply by looking at it wh or not it is needing a drink.

If you find that the plant is dry, take a bucket bowl or if you have several plants use the sink, bu that the water level will come above the rim of the Plunge carefully and watch for a stream of bul which should rise from the soil to the surface o water. Wait until the stream of bubbles stops. Tak the pot plant and stand it on the draining board the sink and clean the outside of the pot. Leave plant to drain.

From this time on, how often any plant will watering will depend entirely upon the plant itself its surroundings. Usually a flowering plant will more than one which has large leaves only. Tes suggested, by pressing with newspaper.

Although most house plants need a certain amou warmth, central heating is not good for them u this can be tempered by humidity. It helps tremenc ly if you can spray the air round a plant and somet its foliage also with clean water from an atomiser. rain water both for watering and spraying if poss This is essential if the mains water contains lime you are growing azaleas and other lime haters.

Fortunately, there is a method of providing hum which also improves the general appearance consequently the decorative value of the pot plai well. This involves plunging the plant pot insi larger cover pot. All kinds of vessels can be usec this purpose and many of these will be those originally intended for horticultural purposes a: shall see. However, one should point out that n flower vases, especially those with a stem or s pedestal base are ideal for this because they lift display the plants so attractively. Most bromeli which are inclined to be top heavy sometimes, look in the urn-type, classic flower vase. Pedestal vase invaluable where a spreading plant is growing in a s flower pot. Unprotected or un-anchored it is likel become easily knocked over.

But to return to the actual plunging. In any of t cover pots – and the term extends to troughs and o large containers, you should pack well-moistened bulb-fibre, sand, moss, old crumbled Oasis which have used for flower arrangements, vermiculite or clean water-retentive material you can find, includ if all else fails, shredded kitchen paper. This pac should go under and around the pot plant, read right up to the rim which should be well below edge of the outer pot, to make watering clean and

Right
Plants sometimes need to be – and can be – kept under control. The Joya at the back of the group, instead of being allowed to climb, has been trained round a hoop. The trailing plectranthus has been kept in a small pot to constrict its growth and the striped cryptanthus has been left to grow into a cluster.

Far right
Caladium hybrids. Caladiums are among the few foliage plants that are very difficult to grow. They rarely survive the winter outside a green-house. They grow from tubers and require plenty of warmth and water freely while they are growing freely.

Right
Epiphyllum hybrid. One of the many lovely flowering cacti known as leaf-flowering—a misnomer because the flowers are really produced on the flattened stems or plant bodies. The main flowering period is from May to June.

Opposite page top
Dieffenbachia picta. There are several species of this plant. They like warm, humid, light conditions but will become adapted to cooler, dryer environments. Stem portions and sap are highly poisonous to humans causing swollen mouth membranes, hence the popular name Dumb Cane.

Opposite page bottom
Watering bromeliads is quite a different operation from caring for other plants. In their case it is important that the little well, vase or reservoir at the heart of the plant and made by the overlapping leaves is always kept filled with water.

The packing or plunge material should be kept moist
[bu]t not sodden. If you use this method you will find that
[pla]nts grow better, even though you do not have to
[wa]ter them so frequently, than if they are simply stood
[in] a saucer with the surface of the pot exposed to the
[dr]ying air. Cacti should not be in a moist plunge but
[so]me succulents, especially the epiphytic kinds, benefit
[fro]m it. Several different kinds of plants can be mixed
[to]gether in a plunge medium but we will discuss this
[mo]re fully when we come to the subject of plant
[arr]angement generally.

[A]lthough plants help to cleanse our atmosphere for
[by] taking in the gases we cannot use and expelling
[pre]cious oxygen, they or at least some of them can
[be]come badly affected by some atmospheric conditions.
[Fu]mes from oil lamps and heaters, from domestic gas
[app]liances, from paint, cleaning fluids, even tobacco
[can] affect some so much that they become ill or even
[die]. Saintpaulias, pelargoniums and cyclamen are
[exa]mples. Generally speaking, once again, the dark
[gre]en tough-leaved kinds are best able to tolerate
[pol]lution and those with thick chunky leaves or plant
[bod]ies such as sansevierias and cacti seldom show
[sig]ns of distress.

[U]nfortunately, we find that just as plants become
[ove]r-watered so do many of them become over-fed.
[W]e should certainly feed plants from time to time
[but] never too generously. Too much plant food can
[kill] so never be tempted to give just a little more. Plants
[pro]ducing flower buds, or those which have been rested
[and] are coming into growth again, usually need feeding
[but] generally speaking they need only sufficient food
[to k]eep them healthy and of good appearance. As a
[rul]e, it is much more convenient for a permanent plant
[to g]row slowly. Plants which grow too fast and con-
[seq]uently too large, can be a nuisance. You have to find
[new] homes for them. By feeding a plant very lightly we
[can] keep it growing in proportion with its environment
[and] to the purpose for which we chose it. It will thrive—
[but] slowly.

[W]e should always remember that plants in our homes
[are] influenced by the amount of artificial light and extra
[war]mth around them and so they cannot be expected
[to b]ehave as they would if they were growing naturally.
[All] plants rest at some time of the year but this period
[of r]est may not necessarily be in winter or, if this is the
[pro]per time for the plant to take its rest, growth might
[con]tinue because artificial light extends the length of
[the] plant's day.

[It] is not difficult to tell whether or not a plant is
[ma]king new growth. If it is winter and you see no signs
[of t]his, do not feed the plant but allow it to rest instead.
[Usu]ally, during these rest periods, you will find that
[plan]ts need less water also. As soon as you see signs of
[new] growth you will find that a little more water is
[nee]ded and once this happens you can give the plant a
[littl]e help by feeding it with a very little soluble plant
[food]. It is best to start very gently by putting just a
[littl]e in the regular water and then you can lead up to
[max]imum amounts should these be necessary, tapering
[off a]gain when you feel that the plant is slowing down.

Plant care

...s that are unhealthy cannot remain decorative for ... and so it follows that if we want them to give us ...alue we should learn how to care for them when ...re healthy and how to tend them when they are ... in some way or other.

...st of all let us make quite sure that we all know ... is meant by watering a plant. This does not mean ...ng a tablespoonful over the surface each morning ...oes it mean allowing a pot to stand in several ...s of water for some hours.

...very pot, bowl or other container, there should be ... area between the top soil or soil surface and the ...rim or edge. Thinking in terms of the flower pots ...selves, this space should be between a $\frac{1}{2}$–1 inch ... 60, and for a 48 more, because more water is ...d for a larger plant. Bear these points in mind ... you repot plants or make dish gardens or plant ... types of containers–you need room to water.

When the plant is watered this area should be filled. If the soil compost is properly mixed and well-drained or open as it should be, and certainly if the soil is dry, the water will be quickly sucked through and, if the plant should be standing in a saucer, you will notice that this quickly fills. This water should not be tipped away but should be left so that the soil and roots can slowly absorb it. If the pot soil is already wet enough the water takes longer to drain through. This may be an indication that you are watering too much or too often. Should this be the case, you can apply a little first aid by standing the pot on some absorbent material, several folds of newspaper for example, so that moisture is drawn out. Allow the soil to become almost quite dry before you water the plant again. Plants which are plunged lose their water into the plunge material and are able to re-absorb it slowly.

Plants in flower are at their peak and usually they need more water at this time. If they are in bud when you buy them, or if you have them young and so watch them come into bud, they should be fed. As we have already learned, plants need humidity and one should remember that a plant in flower has an even greater surface through which precious moisture will be lost if the atmosphere is too dry. If your plants are plunged you may have to water them a little more often than usual, so it is wise to check. Use an atomiser on the plants but keep the spray off the actual flowers in case these are the kind that become discoloured. If your plants are newly bought and are labelled, you may be advised to water freely. It is difficult for me to say just how often this might be necessary because this depends upon the size of the plant, the number of its blooms and where it stands. It might need no more than a weekly watering, on the other hand, some flowering plants in

Left
Aphelandra, begonia and variegated hibiscus. These and many other plants need a high degree of humidity in the home. They are best grown with their pots plunged inside another filled with some moisture-retentive material such as peat. The aphelandra is a beautiful plant; the leaves can be up to ten inches long and it has large yellow flowers set in vase shaped bracts.

Below
Maranta leuconeura. 'Erythrophylla'. Marantas need a warm, moist atmosphere or they will not produce a succession of new leaves. A gentle spray of clean water on the foliage from time to time will help to keep them happy.

Right
Hydrangea. Hydrangeas need
plenty of water and regular
feeding when they are in
flower. Always stand a pot
inside another or in a deep
saucer so that it can be
watered freely and safely.

hot sunny weather, need watering every day.

Some people let the plant pot stand in a puddle of water in a saucer and although this might work sometimes it is not really to be recommended. The soil seldom becomes aerated this way and it is possible for it to become so water-logged that the plant finally dies. Plants should 'paddle' only when directions for their culture include the advice, 'keep the soil constantly moist', examples are the little flowering rush-like *Cyperus*.

It is important to clean plants so that their leaf pores do not become clogged with dust. If it is convenient, stand plants outdoors in a gentle summer shower but guard against wind and torrential rains because these could damage the leaves. If you can spray climbing and large leaved plants in situ, so much the better. To avoid making the soil too wet if you do this, spread a little plastic or a dust sheet over the pot surface.

If leaves have become very dusty one must guard against scratching them with any grit particles which might be in the dust. The best way to clean a really dusty plant is to syringe it so that the dust is washed away. It is possible sometimes to blow the dust by using a vacuum cleaner in reverse, in which case one has to work quickly to suck the dust in from the air immediately after this. Alternatively, carefully sponge the leaves with a sponge, soft cloth or tissue. Use tepid water, try to wash the whole of one surface with one gentle stroke, wipe off the moisture with another drier cloth. If the dust is grimy or greasy as it is sometimes in cities, squeeze a few drops of detergent into the water, use this water and then rinse with untreated water.

Do not smear the leaves with oils or any substance other than water unless this be an insecticide. Pores can so easily be clogged with oils and once this happens the leaf cannot breathe nor work properly and it dies.

House plants sometimes become infested with insects as do garden plants. Quite often these will spread from one plant to the others. Some plants are notoriously dirty, cinerarias for instance. These seem to draw aphis to them. Inspect the undersides of their leaves every day.

Before you decide to buy insecticides and a syringe or atomiser with which to apply them, ask yourself if this is economic – sometimes the cure costs more than a new plant.

Do remember that insecticides are poisons and do not use the spray in the home. The only exceptions are fly-killers designed specifically for domestic use. Incidentally, these are often effective against a mild attack of aphis or greenfly. Otherwise take plants outdoors, out of the wind, spray them and allow them to become dry before you bring them back indoors. Read the labels and follow the directions carefully. Systemic insecticides can save some bother if you add a small dose to the water once a month because this will prevent serious infestations. Certainly use this method once you have sprayed a plant.

Most of the insect pests live by sucking the sap of the plants. This weakens the plant and it also can spread diseases. Systemic insecticides work through the system of the plant. If these are watered into the soil they can be taken up through the roots and then spread through the plant. Their action is not immediate, it might take two or three days before the poison reaches the pest.

If you are not squeamish, often the most effective means of ridding a plant of a pest is to squash it between thumb and finger.

Greenfly usually cluster first on young shoots of plants. You may be first aware of them either because the surface of a windowsill is sticky from their exudations or because spent insect bodies lie like dust under a plant. It is advisable to keep a magnifying glass handy

and to inspect soft-leaved plants frequently. If notice that a leaf has become distorted this also m be a sign of greenfly or some other aphis colony s ing up. Instant action is often effective and the p does not suffer a great deal.

Another reason why humidity is essential in cultivation of happy house plants is that it deters infestations of an unpleasant little mite known as spider. Some house plant owners have never seen little creature for it occurs only when the atmosphe too dry. A badly affected plant will look rusty and will be because of the thousands of tiny red mites really spiders, encased in webs which cover leaves growing tips.

Apart from a plant not looking well, signs tha spider is present are brown even brittle leaves and n shed leaves. The mites usually collect first of all o underside of the leaves and they are almost impos to see with the naked eye. In certain lights it is ea see the web but not always. The standard wa detecting this is to drop a little cigarette ash or to bl little powder onto the underside of a leaf. If this c you will know that the web is there.

Red spider is difficult to eliminate without wetting with some proprietary insecticide. It migh best to discard the plant. If you do this be sure to c wall surfaces, sills, flower pots or containers an throw away soil or plunge materials used for the affe plant.

To prevent your plants from becoming inf make sure that humidity is provided. Spray with c water wherever possible.

Mealy bug is another, milder, nuisance but it c attacks those plants which are difficult to treat instance, it will cluster down between the spines cactus. It is white or greyish and mealy, looking l tiny piece of cotton wool which has become caug the plant. This meal hides a nasty little sucking b relation, I believe, of the cochineal bug. A spra insecticide will not always reach the cracks crevices in which these insects lurk and the best wa remove them is to take some methylated spirit a matchstick and with lots of patience, scrape awa each little tuft.

Incidentally, I find that I can keep large spiny fairly clean by passing the dusting brush of the vac cleaner over them each week. By the same meth suck out dead leaves caught up in the spines of eu bias. Dead leaves often harbour mealy bugs. From to time, gently shake climbing plants such as rhoic to release any leaves which may be caught up in trails.

The most frequent disease seems to be mildew the various kinds of mildews are caused by watering and sometimes a combination of too n water and too little heat. Some mildews affect the s some the leaf surfaces which become covered. C watering also causes wilts and root rots. Plants affected are really best discarded.

Fortunately, in spite of these awful descriptions h plant pests and diseases are relatively few and are or need not be, troublesome in most homes. important thing is to keep watch on the plants ar keep them clean. Sponging and syringing leaves insects almost as much as more drastic measures

Increasing plants

...e are some house plants which lose much of their ...al as they grow older, especially if they have to be ...ned to small pots. Some, like tradescantia become ...gly and lose colour, plectranthus can grow too ...ant and take over a shelf or some corner of a room, ...nia rex varieties can grow much too large for their ... and present an unattractive root portion in the ...e of the plant, an aechmea after it has flowered ...develop so many offsets or daughter plants round ...nain vase that it becomes top-heavy. All of these ...others like them are best replaced by younger, ...r and more vigorous specimens.

...any house plants can be very easily increased by ... means or another. Stem cuttings can be taken ...tradescantia and plectranthus and others and ...will root in moist sand, in cuttings compost and ...in plain water. Large begonia plants and many ...s can be divided into several smaller ones. The ...of the mature begonia leaves can be used as leaf ...ngs and will produce plants. Offsets from aechmea ...many other plants can be detached from the parent ...and grown on individually. There are also other ...ns of propagation, all simple, and within the scope ...e most amateur gardener.

...ose who hope to make many plant arrangements ...ot-et-fleur arrangements will find that a stock of ...l plants will prove invaluable. Sometimes, you can ...cuttings in the place of plants and these can be ...ing roots while they are part of an arrangement. ...ttings are the easiest form of propagation. Often ...ou have to do is to nip off a growing shoot and ...ly push into another pot or into water, it is that ...Cuttings vary considerably; they can be a shoot ...the growing tip of a plant, a section of stem, a ...on of root, a snip of a leaf or a full leaf.

...e tips of some plants, such as tradescantia, ...ranthus, rhoicissus, philodendron, impatiens and ...ra are among the easiest of all. As a rule, the shoot ...t or nipped out about a quarter-inch below a leaf. ...lower leaves or leaf are trimmed off, with scissors ...sharp knife to avoid peeling the stem, in case they ...soil or water and so create a source of infection. ...bare portion of stem is then inserted into whatever ...ng medium is chosen. Usually one should aim to ...at least one third the length of the cutting as a ...ng portion. Hormone rooting powders can be used ...celerate the formation of roots. If you use these, ...w the directions carefully.

...e plants mentioned above can be rooted in plain ...r. Later when puddle-pots are being described, ...names will be added to the list. Rooting compost ...e bought but most cuttings root extremely well in a ...le home-made mixture of half sand and half com-...with a little extra sand as a top layer. Put a few ...es or pebbles in the bottom of the pot first.

If you wish to save space you can plant several cuttings to a pot, inserted round near the rim in a ring. When they are rooted, tip out the root ball very gently and just as gently tease them apart and pot them separately.

Fill the pot, ram the compost down a little because cuttings root better in a firm medium, make a little hole to take the stem with a pencil or skewer. Take it to the required depth, remove and insert the trimmed stem. Push the dibber down at an angle at the side of the cutting so that it is firmed and the hole in which it is set filled at the same time. Give the pot a sharp tap to settle the soil and then water the cuttings.

Rooting mediums should be damp and they should not be allowed to dry out. To keep moisture in you can cover the cuttings in some way, with a jamjar or with a transparent plastic bag for instance. If possible let these covers stay on until the cuttings root. If excessive moisture forms inside the cover, remove it and wipe it dry. A plastic bag needs only to be turned inside out and the dry side is then inside. Should you see mildew forming on any of the leaves, pick them off and give the cuttings more ventilation by taking the cover off for a while each day.

If you strike cuttings in water you can easily see when the roots have formed. If the cuttings are in pots give them a gentle tug at any time after two or three weeks to see if they are anchored or not.

For those who enjoy indoor gardening, taking leaf cuttings can be rewarding in more ways than one. Actually, a great many house plants can be propagated this way but not in the casual manner I am about to describe. Most will need the warm, close, humid atmosphere of a special propagating frame, most practical to run in a greenhouse although it is possible to buy small electrically heated frames for use in a home.

Begonia rex leaves, or those of other types are extremely easy and the satisfying thing about these is that you can use them first in flower arrangements and then as cuttings. Insert the leaf with its entire stem under the water into a little vessel. This can be glass or opaque, it does not seem to matter. After some days roots will emerge from the stem base and then a little later a tiny cluster of miniature leaf buds will begin to develop at

Left
Fibrous-rooted begonias and some of the new tuberous-rooted varieties are easily raised from seed in a warm place. They are all very free-flowering and bloom for months on end.

Above
Chlorophytum elatum 'Variegatum'. The little plantlets produced at the tips of the arching flowering stems can be encouraged to make individual mature plants. These can each be directed into a pot of soil. When it has grown into this the plantlet can be detached from its parent plant. Plantlets can also be detached and rooted in water.

the junction of stem and leaf. Soon these grow into leaves and eventually you have a beautiful new young plant which often retains its mother leaf for a long time.

Peperomias, saintpaulias or African violets and gloxinias will root easily this way in the home. If you want to try others, take them and keep the cutting inside a glass storage jar or a transparent plastic bag in good light and in a warm place–even on a shelf over a radiator which is not a place I would usually recommend for plants. All of these can also be rooted in compost.

Another method of taking begonia cuttings is to divide the leaf in such a way that the leaf bud clusters are formed in several places on its surface. Lay the leaf face downwards on the table and cut through the thickest veins with a sharp knife making cuts of about a $\frac{1}{2}$ inch from one side to the other. The cuts should be

made at the point where the veins divide and on the side nearest the stem. Retain the stem – or at least about an inch of it.

Have ready a 50–50 mixture of peat and sand in a seed pan, flower pot saucer, special little propagating tray with plastic lid which you can buy for this purpose and for raising seeds or, and this I use, a shallow plastic food container with a transparent lid.

Holding the slashed leaf carefully in the palm of your hand, turn it the right way up. Gauge its length and make a hole for the short stem. Insert this as you lay the leaf flat. See that the leaf lies flat on the moist compost, weight it down here and there if necessary with a little more, just a pinch will do.

Plantlets should spring from the cut areas. Cover the box or pan with glass or transparent plastic. When the plantlets are well formed pot them up.

Some plants produce plantlets without being goaded into action this way. Some ferns form plantlets on fronds, some succulents on their leaves or like the bryophyllum in a delightful fringe round the margin of a leaf. These plantlets may be potted and will grow into large plants.

Other plants send out plantlets on the ends of runners or stolens. These remain on the parent plant until the little plantlet finds a home for itself and then the runner gradually rots away. In the home, we can direct these

stolons to drop their plantlets on a pot of soil ready waiting. Here the little plantlet will soon grow into the soil and all you have to do is to snip the umbilical cord. Chlorophytums send out a number of these stolons which add to the attractiveness of the plant. Often you will see the thick thong-like roots forming while they dangle in the air.

A similar method may be used for layering plants. In this case, one leads a good trail of any climber to a pot of soil, or even to a vessel of water. The stem is held down on the soil or in the water – a stone is usually the best means, just lay this over the stem so that it stays in place, and roots should grow from the part of stem which comes in contact with the rooting medium. Often roots grow quicker into soil if the skin of the stem is scraped away at this point.

Air-layering is a means of renewing, even tidying some plants. As varieties of *Ficus decora*, dieffenbachias and dracaenas grow older often the tuft of leaves is borne higher and higher on the tip of a stem which has become a trunk. As a rule the plants are not attractive so unless there is a special reason for keeping a tall plant it is best to air-layer the portion of plant at the top of the trunk.

At a point a few inches below the lowest leaf and with a sharp knife, mark a circle round the stem by cutting through the skin. Mark another circle about a $\frac{1}{2}$ inch. lower down. It should now be possible to peel the skin away from this area. This should now be covered with some material into which roots, which should spring from the cut portion, will grow. Traditionally, moist sphagnum moss is used, a handful say about the size of a tennis ball, spread round the stem and then tied to it and finally covered with plastic to cut down loss by evaporation. Should you find it difficult to buy the moss, use a small cylinder of Oasis, cut down the centre. Soak this in water and then take the two halves and place them on each side of the stem. Press them against the stem and bind them in place and cover them the same way as you would cover the moss.

The piece of plastic – sheeting or even a clear bag will do – should be tied firmly both above and below the rooting medium. It is prudent to examine it after a few days to ensure that all is keeping moist.

Once you can see the roots through the plastic, the new plant can be severed from its parent stem. Rather than damage the new roots, pot the whole mass, i.e. moss or plastic and roots together.

You can see when a plant needs repotting often without knocking it from its pot. Turn it upside down and see if any roots are roaming through the drainage holes. With other plants, it is quite obvious that they are bursting their bonds and that not even a move into a larger pot will really benefit them. Primulas, some ferns, chlorophytums, aspidistras, begonias, impatiens are a few examples which come quickly to mind. Sometimes, and this is expecially the case with ferns and with large epiphyllums and aechmeas, the roots are so massed, that one can do no more than to cut the root mass into great chunks each with its own topknot of leaves. Others can be tipped out and sections simply teased out from the mass. Keep the new pots on the small side, just large enough to take the new root portion comfortably.

After dividing or repotting plants treat them a little tenderly. Water them in, as this settles the soil round their roots, but avoid giving them too much water, give them time to make new roots first. Spray them overhead so that their leaves are kept moist instead if this is practicable. Keep them in good light but out of the sun, even if they are sun lovers.

Flower Arranging

Containers

les of arrangements for flowers in the home ly are based on the position or place in which the rs are to stand, though of course, the flowers or materials which are used are themselves bound to a great influence on the patterns into which they rranged. Obviously, if one wants flowers, heavy and wayward leaves to remain in the position place designated for them, one should employ means of holding them secure. For this purpose se stem holders. There are types to suit every ose, as we shall see. Possibly the easiest to find and nly the most adaptable and the cheapest is large wire-netting.

e finds this indispensable not only as a stem holder owers, when it can be cut to fit any vase, but also naking cones to be studded with evergreens or rs, for making pockets or nests to take fruits and ds which are part of an arrangement but which

should not be in water, and as we have already learned, as a prop, wedge, heightener and support for plant arrangements. In fact, once he or she begins to use wire-netting, the flower arranger will find that it is often the answer to some decorative problem. For instance, certain shapes can be cut out from the netting and then decorated.

Small-mesh wire is not suitable because it is so stiff. Use large-mesh wire: $1\frac{1}{2}$–2 inch mesh is best for flower arrangements because the wire is so pliable and will give as a stem passes through it, yet remain firm enough to hold the stems where you want them. If it is necessary to make an outsize arrangement in which the stems are really tall and tapering, cut a little more netting than usual and after filling the vase take several inches up above the rim of the vase. Place the tallest stem in position wrapping some of the netting, at the back of the container, round the base of its stem until it is secure. One can anchor great boughs of leaves and blossoms or tall stems of such subjects as pampas grass this way.

The usual method is to cut a piece of netting which measures twice the height of the container and a little more than its width. The netting is then crumpled up or bent U-shaped and inserted into the mouth of the container.

Some vases and other containers are so much easier to fill with flowers than others. Waisted vases or those that flute out at the rim and then become very narrow to the base are usually difficult to fill. It is certainly awkward to make some flowers in them fall prettily at a low angle. The way to deal with these is not to attempt to fill the vase with netting from the base to the rim, as is usual, instead, just measure the top width and set the netting in this area only.

This also is the method for using glass containers.

Previous pages
Double narcissi and tulips, hyacinths, leucocoryne and eucalyptus. When the arrangement is to be viewed from the front only, and not from all angles, the centre stem should be placed well back to allow room for many flowers in front of it.

Left
Carnations, roses, chrysanthemums and schizostylis (kaffir lilies) with mixed foliage and honesty. One vase stands inside another to make this deep arrangement. The top pedestal vase is filled with wire-netting and a ring of netting inside the lower vase encircles its foot.

Below left
Ornamental gourds, single chrysanthemums and elaeagnus foliage. Full of colour and exciting texture, a group of flowers, fruit and foliage makes an attractive decoration. Large fruits can be stood, like eggs in a cup, in jars which are easily hidden by the other components.

Below
'Apricot Silk' roses in glass. Because the neck of the glass is small most of these roses were arranged and tied in the hand. The two lower blooms were arranged separately. They wedge the bunch into position and hide the tie.

Secure a smaller piece of wire-netting in the mouth of the glass only. If you have doubts about its stability, secure it in a few places, and on the outside of the glass where it will not become damp, with a few strips of adhesive tape. The flower stems can then pass down through the netting which will hold them as you wish, into the water, while the means of holding the stems is hidden. You can always arrange a few leaves or flowers below rim level so as to hide the least trace of the netting.

When using glass containers, put in a nugget or two of charcoal to keep the water clear. If, however, the water becomes cloudy as it does sometimes during very hot weather, do not disturb your arrangement but take it to the sink, part the stems a little at the back of the arrangement and let a cold tap run with force into the vessel. This will change the water and aerate it at the same time.

When you push the netting into any container, push the folded end in first and hold the netting so that the ends of the cut edge are uppermost. These can be used to advantage. You can crook them over a rim to hold the

ight mixture of annuals
with a shoot from a pot
is arranged in a bowl
g on a flat green
l dish. Low-lying
hide the water vessel.

onies, delphiniums,
scotch mist, sweet peas
ks. The contrasting
of the full blooms and
key delphiniums give
angement fullness and
on.

er jelly mould keeps
ool and sweet and
a lively and natural air
imple garden flowers.

netting firm – do this in three or four places if necessary. You can also use these little snag ends to embrace any very tall stems that need to be more restrained than others or which are heavy or inclined to turn about as some do, the forced guelder rose is an example.

If you want to make some stems hang down really low below rim level you can do this by hooking an end or two round them quite near rim level where the wire will not show. You can then exert gentle but firm pressure on the wire until the stems fall into the position you want. At other times these wire ends can be pushed through a stem, just as though they were pins. This will hold a stem just where you want it and yet do it no harm.

To return for a moment to glass containers. You can dispense with wire-netting altogether for these if you wish to arrange just one lovely branch or perhaps a group of flowers flowing at some special angle in the oriental manner.

Obviously whatever method you use, the important thing is that the holder should not show through the glass. It is possible, when you are using a narrow necked glass – or an opaque vase – to wedge one stem, or a very few stems, in place by pushing short, thick pieces of bare stem between the branch and the side of the container.

You can also use a lump of modelling clay the same way but if you do, remember that clay will stick only to perfectly dry surfaces so get it in place and the stem arranged before adding the water.

Simple and effective are the ancient Japanese 'kubari', either the forked or cross stick type. Kubari should always be cut from living twigs, cupressus is excellent for this purpose. First cut the twig so that it fits tightly in the mouth of the container. This may not necessarily be across the widest portion because the stem may look best flowing from some point near the rim, so test first. Split the wood and wedge it open with another small piece of the same twig so that it resembles a Y.

Cross twigs should first be measured in the same way and then simply fastened together at the centre with raffia or fine twine.

A very modern form of kubari is simply to cut a block of Oasis, about which I have more to say later, and wedge this in the mouth of the container.

Another effective way to hold one single stem, a branch of blossom for instance, is to bend but not break the base of the stem so that it makes a 'foot' at right angles to the main stem. This should fit snugly from one side of the base of the container to the other. This being

Previous pages
Poppy anemones. Buy or
pick *Anemone coronaria*
flowers before they open,
but not too young, or they
will not mature. To keep a
bowl going, add a few buds
each week and remove only
those flowers which drop their
petals.

Horse chestnut blossoms
can sometimes be heavy and a
little difficult to control. Pieces
of driftwood at the centre of
this arrangement hold the
stems in place and also form
part of the design.

Right
Chincherinchees and copper
beech. Pinholders are suitable
for arrangements in the
oriental style. Stems are
impaled on or across the
points. Leafy laterals pruned
from the main stem hide the
stem-holder and add to the
general effect of the arrangement.

Opposite page
Daffodils, aucuba and
chlorophytum leaves with a
giant sea-snail shell. Shells of
all kinds can be used in many
ways in flower arrangements.
This shell conceals the
pinholder. At the same time it
emphasises the curving lines
of the design. The deep green
leathery leaves of the aucuba
make very useful foliage
additions.

so the branch will stay upright and firmly in place.

An invaluable aid is the pinholder which holds stems impaled upon its points. Woody stems can be cut on a slant, or even split and then can be arranged at almost any angle. Pinholders come in all shapes and sizes. You can buy one, or a series of them, small enough and dainty enough for a wineglass. Actually, these little holders can be pressed against the side of a glass to hold one stem. Other pinholders are so large that they are heavy to lift but they are invaluable for holding a really heavy branch in place inside the vase.

Although they can be used inside a tall vessel, pin-holders are most useful for arrangements made in shallow containers. It is important that the pinholder does not move or slip about if the arrangement is moved. To prevent this happening simply make three or four peasized pills of modelling clay and press them under the *dry* holder. Do this lightly but firmly so that they adhere but are still rounded. Then turn the holder right way up and press it down on the container in the spot in which it is to stand. As the pills are flattened they provide a bond between the two which can later be easily removed.

If you would like to use a dish or a plate or some other object which is really too shallow to hold water, use a tin or small deeper supplementary container to hold the water and the pinholder. Place the clay pills under the water vessel as well as under the pinholder in this case.

Foamed plastic stem holders, such as Oasis, are great aids to the flower arranger. Made of foamed urea, their texture is soft, sponge-like and unresistant. They are available the world over.

Probably the most important thing about them is that you can so easily insert a stem into the surface where it will immediately hold firm. If the stem is very short, you need insert no more than 1 inch or even less. As you will appreciate, this is a great advantage because many lovely subjects, leaves in particular, are often very short stemmed. Should you wish, and you might if you were making Christmas decorations, you can even insert stems upside down and they will still stay in place.

Because the plastics absorb and hold water they can be used ex-container, that is to say, on a plate rather than inside a vessel. However, when it is used this way one should realise that the moisture will evaporate constantly and that the plastic will need re-soaking each day.

When used inside a container it is most convenient to put a square peg in a round hole, in other words, a rectangular block in a cylindrical vessel. This then leaves four spaces near the rim, and water can be poured into whichever one is most conveniently placed.

Obviously, it is a great advantage to have a variety of stem holders but where the arranger is working to a limited budget and in cases of emergency it is possible to devise many simple means of holding stems. Long ago, wet clay, straws bunched and pressed into a vase, and box snippets arranged to come just to rim level, were some of the means employed. The important thing is to ensure that the stem holder is so firmly wedged or anchored that it cannot move while the flowers are being arranged. As a rule, it is the first few stems that need most careful placement. Once these stand firm and as required, other stems which cross them below rim level inside the vase become locked and these then make a stem holder for those which follow.

For those who have no pinholders a large potato offers a good substitute on occasions. Its base should be sliced so that it holds firm. Woody stems can be cut on a slant and thrust into this. Larger holes can be made

with a peeler or an apple corer to take small and stemmed flowers which should be bunched before The potato is hidden with a cluster of stones also anchor it.

Those new to flower arranging may find it intere to note that hiding the stem holder in a low arrange often anchors the flowers in such a way that they be welded to the container. And the way one decid camouflage a stem holder can add to the interest arangement as a whole. Often it is sufficient simp arrange the largest leaves or flowers so low that alth they are not actually in the water they are so near t surface that they screen the holder. If the arrange is in a vertical style to do this may not be right and one resorts to the use of shells, stones, small gr pieces of driftwood, cork, bark, fungi—these c dried and used again and again, actually, any na material which has some beauty or interest to com it. Pet shops stock certain items which make accessories, coral, rocks, sea-fans.

Where it is essential that objects are kept o water it is usually a simple matter to lay a pie bark, plastic, cork or even a flat shell, across the tainer from one side to the other near the pinh and to arrange them on this. Wire-netting can be as a nest for the same purpose and in this case on use leaves to hide it and place the other things on t

Wire-netting can be cut and rolled to make a Cut out a paper pattern first. The base can be pushe the container and the flowers inserted all ove surface of the wire shape, through the netting, stems down into the water. Alternatively, a cone c stuffed with moss or damp foamed plastic. Howev is much simpler, especially if you are making se Christmas decorations, to buy the foamed p shapes ready-made for this purpose. These con several sizes. They are also available in spherical These can be used to make floral bosses which can be mounted on a stem like a little tree-trunk or pended from a cord or ribbon.

Styles

kinds of annuals fill this
...ian vase designed for
...vels of flowers. The tall
...shaped container fits
... the bowl. One can
...vise similar containers
...everyday objects quite

...ns and driftwood.
...al flowers fit naturally
...ormal patterns but there
...any simple ways we can
...duce a little informality
...ut diminishing their
...veness. Driftwood adds
...s and hides the stem
...r.

...nculus in a Queen conch
...There is really no limit
... type of containers you
...se. So long as whatever
...ould like to use can
...vater or some moisture-
...ive material it will do.
... and flowers go
...ifully together.

One of the best pieces of advice I can give relating to flower arrangement is this: don't be tied in any way. Don't think that you have to have special vases, that you have to follow special rules, that you have to use only certain kinds of flowers, materials or colours. The way you arrange flowers should depend entirely on how you want to see them. However, I think that it needs stressing that flower arrangement proper means value for money and reward for time spent, which the mere placement of flowers can never be. Think in terms of buying a few beautiful flowers and spinning them out with foliage and other accessories. Collect a wide range of containers because these will help you ring the changes constantly and you can elect to use the same cheap flowers for weeks on end without ever becoming tired of them. Collect containers with the same liberal point of view as I suggested you should adopt when looking for those suitable for plant ar-

ft
you have some fine leaves
en you need only a few
wers to furnish a vase.
ese are from the shrub
ododendron falconeri and
ve velvety undersides which
rmonise with the orange
rysanthemums 'Galaxy'.

ow left
rysanthemums, kale and
ch leaves and briza grass
a wooden knifebox.
e attractive-looking fruit
still be taken from this dish.
it is replaced the colours
the decoration may change
ttle but not the character.

rangements. Apart from true flower vases—and so far as these are concerned do realise that some of these are difficult to use, especially the old fashioned types which need so many flowers to fill them attractively—you can use anything that holds water or which can be made to appear to do so.

If you make a collection of accessories for flower arrangements you will always have a source of decoration and of inspiration. These with your house plants will ensure that you can always rustle up a flower arrangement or a party decoration for some special occasion. Do remember that anything that grows can be used. Driftwood is particularly lovely for this purpose and it is worth while searching the beach to find one piece or more that is beautifully shaped, no

matter how small. If you find only small pieces they can be joined together quite effectively to make a piece which is shaped more to your liking. Such pieces can be given false stems or they can simply be laid or wedged in place.

Cone and certain seed heads, such as poppy, lotus, morning glories, proteas, camphor tree pods, all on sale at certain times of the year, will look like wooden flowers. You can arrange these with fresh materials as well as dried ones.

Most things lifted from the fruit bowl or the vegetable basket will look well arranged with flowers and leaves. Those crisp, vivid yellow coral-curly leaves from the forced rhubarb, large parsley leaves, especially if they are yellowing a little, frost-blue outer leaves of cabbage,

even a whole little cabbage can play a part.

Many leaves will eke out a few flowers and give substance as well as beauty to an arrangement. Fern fronds and fallen leaves, picked up in the park perhaps, can be used fresh and then pressed and kept for some other occasion. If you have a vigorous leafy house plant, borrow a leaf or two from it. If possible, select those which you know you can treat as leaf cuttings after they have served their term in the decorations, the beautifully coloured leaves of *Begonia rex* are ideal for this purpose. Use trails of tradescantia, ivies, plectranthus and rhoicissus with all uniform flowers which could do with a little informality and root the cuttings afterwards.

A fruit bowl can become a flower arrangement with such little effort. Put a piece of well soaked Oasis in a waterproof plastic bag and hide it among the fruit. This will hold the flower and leaf stems. If necessary use two or more of these containers so that you can distribute the flowers well. Generally speaking, shiny blooms look better and cleaner with fruit than do those with soft petals. You can also use children's party balloons filled with water or tablet tubes to hold the flower stems as we do in pot-et-fleur arrangements.

The lovely texture of gladioli can take any of the brightest fruits, for none of these are likely to overpower the flowers themselves. This is a good way to use these flowers when they have past their best and the spike is no longer the complete beautiful thing it was. Snap off the tip on which there are still good florets and renew these by arranging them in a completely different manner. This is one example of what I mean about studied flower arrangement being value for money.

In its widest sense, flower arrangement falls roughly into two groups, formal—into which group fall the traditional arrangements, and informal. There are subdivisions of these groups. Generally speaking, the type of flowers often, but not always, guide us as to what style to use. As you will appreciate, uniform flowers, especially where only one kind is to be used in an arrangement, tend to fall into formal patterns. Indeed, so far as shop flowers are concerned, their perfect uniformity is often best exploited.

In our homes, we find that certain styles suit one place better than another. For example, on a table that stands in the centre of a room or round which people pass the flowers should be arranged so that they look good from any angle.

Decorations of this kind are called, for want of a better name, all-round arrangements. For a sideboard or for a decoration that has to be set against a wall it is necessary only to face the flowers so that they look out into the room. Actually this is a very economic style because you will not need so many flowers. These are known as faced arrangements.

On these two themes we can play many variations. Flowers for special little places about the home may not need to conform to any particular style any more than any other ornament in the house. These can be made truly pictorial or scenic. Alternatively, they can be sparse and oriental in style, expecially if some furnishing or other decoration nearby is in the same mood.

So far as traditional styles are concerned, think in terms of shapes, the shapes which you would get if you were to draw a line round the flowers' tips after they were arranged. This may sound complicated to a beginner but it is true to say that after doing only very few flower arrangements one can see how these shapes emerge, and by the same token, one can quickly appreciate which are likely to be the most suitable for one's own needs.

Let us take first a bowl of flowers arranged for a table

Previous page
Single chrysanthemums, daffodils, holly, cotoneaster, mistletoe and leucothoe. Strong colour contrasts are warm and welcoming in winter and at Christmas also. The forced daffodils should be bought or picked in bud for a longer vase life.

Top left
Mixed dahlias with parsley, fennel heads and santolina buttons. Short-stemmed flowers look well massed in a simple manner. Even so, each one should be arranged separately. Wire-netting holds these blooms in such a way that each one can be fully admired.

Above
Marigolds in a bowl raised on a pedestal. Like some other flowers, tulips and Iceland poppies for example, marigolds tend to go their own way in an arrangement. Vary stem lengths to give each bloom space to display itself.

Left
Tulips, freesias, hyacinths and mimosa in a work basket. Wickerwork and flowers go well together. Either line the basket with foil or plastic or install a water-tight container, a tin for instance. Prop the lid open before arranging the flowers.

73

si in variety, tulips,
hyacinths and guelder
Viburnum opulus, red-
maple and broom tips
lecups. When making a
arrangements do them
er (arranging one stem
at a time) so as to make
wins. Candlecup designs
ese can be used with
lowers at any season of
ar. The all-round shape
e-centre arrangements is
ularly important.

See following page.

centre. Here you have the choice of several shapes. Which one you select will depend upon the size of the table and the occasion. If no one is to sit at the table the arrangement could be high, wide and handsome. But, if you were arranging the flowers for a dinner table it would be best and more polite, to keep them low. A small table needs only a small decoration at its centre while a very long table could have flowers along most of its length – or perhaps a line of three or five bowls.

The pattern most often used is a half-sphere or globe which is resting in its container which may itself be another half-sphere but this is not essential. This pattern can also be made in a rectangular trough.

As a variation, the side flowers may be elongated so that their arrangement is in the shape of an egg sliced through the centre. In a different manner, the tallest stem may be much longer than the side stems and the intermediate stems adjusted accordingly and then you have a cone.

No matter which of these three basic patterns you select, there is one rule to remember for all-rounders if you want to learn to do them quickly and effectively.

The centre stem should always be plumb in the middle of the container and it should be the only stem that is upright. This is where you will find the little wire-netting cut end hooks so useful. They help to make a bent stem upright. Hook one or two round the stem where it stands up from the netting and gently press on

the wire until the flower head or the tip of the stem is dead centre. After this, every other stem which is arranged should lean away from this central stem even if the angle is only very slight.

The side stems, which should be arranged next, should be at a really wide angle to the centre stem. While the centre stem defines the height of the finished arrangement, the side stems will define its width, and all the other stems should be kept within these dimensions.

For formal faced arrangements, imagine that we slice an all-rounder down the centre so that it becomes a semi-circle, a half oval or a triangle in outline. The centre stem is still the only one that is perpendicular but now it is moved to take up a central position but, this time, as far back against the rim of the container as possible. This is so as to leave plenty of room for all the flowers that are to be placed before it.

Flower arrangements need to have depth and this is an easy way to achieve this effect. Given so much space in front of this centre stem you will be able to arrange the blooms at different levels and to recess some, thus adding to the general interest and avoiding a flat over-formal surface.

Once again all the stems which follow this centre stem placed well back against the rim should lean away from it either to the left or the right, as the case may be. Stems should never be seen to cross each other above rim level. Instead, try to make every stem appear as though it had sprung from a source at the base of this centre stem.

If you can, let the decoration taper at the edges. If you have twelve or ten flowers almost identical and little else to arrange with them, you will find this impossible – one reason why I suggest that it is helpful to collect some accessories. Where flowers seem too much alike, introduce contrast of shape, slender stems such as grass, gladioli leaves, pencil rushes, small-leaved ivy trails, or the spike like flowers of a delphinium. However, even if you have only a bunch of flowers all exactly alike you can still create a flowing or growing effect.

The all-round arrangements just described were for bowls and fairly low containers but there are occasions when this type of arrangement has to be made in a tall container. In such cases one simply follows the same procedure.

To avoid a squat appearance or one in which the container appears to dominate the arrangement, try to make the central stem at least one and a half times the height of the container when measured from the point where it rises from the rim. If by doing this – and because you have no choice of container – you find that the arrangement would be too tall for a table centre, adjust the proportions by making the tallest stem reach the required height and arrange the side stems and all the lowest materials so that they flow over the rim and down the sides and so conceal the true height of the container.

Many arrangements in low shallow vessels have the flavour of the orient about them even if they do not precisely conform to the rules of the ancient and traditional Japanese flower arrangements. These were very strict but even in today's styles they can be helpful. You may not be sufficiently attracted to true Japanese styles to want to copy them but you may find that by studying the principles which underline them you could benefit greatly for they are based on observation and sound common sense.

The basic shape is an irregular triangle and quite often there are only three flowers or stems in an arrangement. These are known as *shushi*. If additonal stems are used these are known as *jushi* and when they are arranged they are always placed within the pattern,

Previous pages left
'Super Star' roses match scarlet sweet peas. Styles flower arrangements hav be based on the role of t arrangement itself. Those which are to stand on a c table should be low so as to be in the way. Howeve you will still need some l stems to obtain the lengt this arrangement – remem to check that all stems ar water all the time.

Previous pages right
Delphiniums, roses, anth and gypsophila in copper When round flowers are massed, use spicate shap taper the edges of the arrangement. As well as delphiniums, grasses, rus leaves and sprays of folia blossom and berries can I used.

Above left
Lilies and driftwood. The method one uses to camo a stemholder can add to interest of the arrangeme as a whole. Three small p of driftwood, carefully pl here look like one wonde contorted piece.

Left
Gladioli and desert spoor Really the bases of faded agave stems, desert spoon are just one example of th many natural, long-lastin plant materials that one c buy or collect to use in fl arrangements.

Right
The fleur-de-lys outline o irises is so lovely that one should give each flower r to display itself. Their uniformity is softened by curving driftwood which helps to hold the shell in place.

outline or dimensions set by the *shushi*.

These three main stems are said to represent heaven, earth and man, *shin*, *soe* and *hikae*. The important stem is *shin* and this one should always be the tallest. It should also be curved and its tip should always be over its base. No matter how curving or undulating this stem might be it is controlled by this rule. The next in importance is *soe* and this second stem is placed to the side of the main stem, and indeed, as it rises from the surface of the water or from the rim of a tall container, it runs so close to *shin* that the two look like one stem. After a little space *soe* should move away to follow

its own way but it must never reach more than two-thirds the height of *shin*. *Hikae* is the lowly stem, as befits its name. It should always occupy a low position in an arrangement. It should flow forward but never downward.

When *jushi* are used, these are always added last, and as a rule just three or five are considered sufficient.

From this basic traditional style many others have evolved and even break-away groups have evolved their own styles also and so it is not possible to speak of one modern Japanese style. Apart from the rigid rules, which not everyone appreciates, the value of these

do not slavishly have to
w Japanese rules to
te a similar delicate and
quil mood in our own
ngements. Here the soft
of winter flowering peach,
ully pruned, frame a few
Christmas roses or
bores, their white petals
rasted against the deep
leaves.

right
t peas and petunias, both
hich are quite long lasting
y are gathered young
gh. The first should have
the lower flower on a
open wide. Petunia buds
d be well coloured.

ight
t peas in a Wedgwood
ort. Cut or buy sweet
with at least one bud
o open. Arrange them in
w water or in foamed
c. Petals must be kept
r the flowers will rot,
ake off rain or dew before
ing them indoors.

an hyacinths, Christmas
(*Helleborus niger*) and
le tulips. With only 1 inch
of their stem ends in
, these hyacinths are
hed to their limit. This
ust a handful of flowers
ake a good-sized
ation. Water should be
d up daily.

lies in the fact that they teach one to use very few
 's. This is a contrast to western traditional flower
 gement in which masses of flowers were and are
 but it is important to stress that you do not have
 ow the rules of Japanese flower arrangements to
 attractive decorations in which only few blooms
 ed.

en we use few flowers we concentrate on the
 y of line. For those who have to buy all their flowers
 rrangements are both fun and quick to assemble.
 stance, for a quick and attractive arrangement,
 five irises, daffodils or any uniform flower.
 ge the flowers in your hand so that each bloom
 s a little above the other. Cut the stem ends level.
 them on a pinholder in a low dish. Move each
 lightly away from its fellow to give it room to
 At the foot of the stems and to hide the holder,
 ge leaves, shells, fruit, seed pods, coral, whatever
 ave. To make a simple variation on this theme
 ge the stems on the holder so that the flowers form
 e, a crescent or an S. This curving line need not be
 it. There may be occasions when you think that it
 l look better flowing to left or right.

Arrangements in which a branch, bare, leafy, berried,
blossomed or lichen-covered, or even driftwood, is
featured with a few flowers can look very lovely in spite
of the fact that they are also very economical. Choose a
branch for its own sake, the more twisted and curved
the better. Failing this, prune a fairly straightforward
branch so that it assumes more the character you want.

For such arrangements, set the pinholder in the dish
either in the centre or to one side—often the latter is
more effective. Set the branch on the pinholder and
then begin to work on it. Pull at the stem gently until
the tip is over the centre of the base of the container and
only when you get this to your satisfaction begin to
introduce other materials. As we have already seen,
the manner in which you hide the pinholder can contribute to the effectiveness and beauty of the whole
arrangement.

If you buy foliage to eke out your flowers you will
find that most branches are too heavy, too dense or the
wrong shape. These need breaking down and dividing
and even then you are likely to find that some foliage
needs removing. Often the leaves you remove can be
used elsewhere.

Opposite page
Iceland poppies (*Papaver
nudicaule*) and briza grasses.
Some flowers, including all
poppies, are best cut in bud,
just before they are ready to
open. They will then last
many days in water. Poppies
should always have their stem
ends singed before they are
arranged to prevent loss of
latex.

Left
Poppy anemones, physalis
(Chinese lanterns), adiantum
fern, holly, clematis seed,
blue spruce and autumn
coloured foliage. There are
only three fresh flowers in this
arrangement. The added value
of an arrangement such as this
is that you can keep it going
for weeks if you change the
water regularly and remove
and replace the flowers as they
fade.

81

stand them in luke-warm water – baby-bath heat, f
least an hour, longer if possible. Those which are n
badly flagging and any which have been stood in
warm water but which have obviously not taken
should be stood in 2–3 inches of boiling water. Let
remain there until the water has cooled and then arr
them in unboiled but luke-warm water. There
exceptions, never stand bulb or corm flowers suc
narcissi, tulips, lilies or gladioli in hot water. The s
will just collapse. Always stand paeonies, delphini
chrysanthemums, scabious, pyrethrums and
annuals in hot water to begin with.

Frail, delicate-looking flowers such as annual gy
phila and saponaria and fern fronds and small-le
soft subjects such as maple are best drawn throug
water, shaken gently to remove surplus moisture
then arranged. Very young and immature foliage
needs immersing for a few minutes, but if you bu:
it should already be hardened or conditioned.

Stems that bleed, that is, exude a white sticky
or latex, can be sealed best and most quickly by pu:
the cut stem into sand, but of course this is not al
handy. It is possible also to stem bleeding by pu:
a little dry Oasis on to the wound. You must trea
stem again if you cut it shorter when arranging. P
of this nature include the poinsettia.

It should not be necessary to change the water
day for flower arrangements. What is important is
there should be no vegetation under the water excer
stem. Leaves, except those of tough evergreens, qu
decompose and turn the water smelly. Even the
greens will rot in time if they are left under water
enough. Always strip the leaves from any portion of
which is to go under water. A word of warning, d
overdo this or you may find that there is a very
zone above the rim of the vase. Top up with fresh v
each day.

Take care though that no leaf touches the v
while its tip is over or on the rim of the cont:
because this might create a siphon and you will
find a pool of water on some precious piece of furn
and an empty vase.

Some flowers last best in shallow water. If you
had gladioli that snap their stems after arrange
they are probably getting too much water. Just
3 inches is sufficient for them and most other bu
corm flowers. Forced tulips however, need a deep c
before arrangement. Sweet peas last best in bow
shallow water than in deep vases although if thes
all you have they can hold a little rather than a l
water.

A lump of sugar or a teaspoonful to a pint of v
will help to feed flowers and keep them looking l
for a little longer than usual. You can also use a
spoonful of honey to a pint of water or even a glu
tablet. Most of the proprietary life-lengtheners
sugar in them and are well worth using if you are
budgeting very carefully. An aspirin tablet or a co
coin really does help the flowers to live longer bec
both help to check bacterial activity. Flowers
longer in metal containers for the same reason.
evergreens and branches you hope to force into
blossom, use a few drops of liquid plant food or a
of a plant food tablet in the water to keep them g
Do not stand glass vessels in a window or in sun
or the water will soon be so active that the flowe
holds will die.

Although it helps some flowers and plants t
lightly sprayed with clean water from an atom
others will simply discolour if water falls on their pe
Fortunately, these are not numerous, most prone
all kinds of violas and sweet peas.

Often one bunch of flowers can be broken up to
make several arrangements which contain three, four
or five flowers. The effect of the arrangement will
depend on the placement of the blooms and the accessories. These do not necessarily have to be arranged
in low containers. For instance, three tall chrysanthemums can be arranged, one above another in a tall
vase with a flurry of some other materials at rim level,
perhaps some berried bunches, leaf clusters, or even a
bunch of some other flowers, say a posy of scarlet
anemones, depending upon the colours used.

Three flowers of medium length can be given height
by using branches, pencil rushes, gladioli leaves placed
behind them. If these are all arranged in a tall vase the
desired effect will be even greater.

One way to save both time and flowers is to make a
permanent framework of leaves before which you can
arrange a few flowers helped out with fruits, foliage or
whatever you can find. As the fresh blooms fade, these
can be easily replaced, even with a different kind of
flower altogether. Some foliage is so long-lasting that
such an arrangement can stay in position for weeks. In
spring you can adopt the same principle but with
different materials, using burgeoning blossom and
spring flowers with perhaps, a flowering house plant or
two.

There are some flowers that flag or wilt badly,
examples are pyrethrums, hot-house roses, forced
tulips, yet once we can get them to take water they perk
up and last well. Almost always the cause of flagging
is an airlock which forms in the stem and this affects
some flowers more than others. Usually the woodiest
or the most fibrous stems, such as stocks, are the most
temperamental.

Never begin arranging flowers as soon as you get
them home except all narcissi. These have tough, hollow
stems and even if the flowers are a little dry and flagged
they quickly drink and perk up.

When flowers have been out of water for some time,
often really hot water treatment is best. Otherwise,

Dried Flowers

...s possible to preserve certain foliage so that it keeps ...ape and general character. Usually the colours ...ge; deep green laurel, for instance, becomes a warm ...nut brown, but this is never a disadvantage. There ...s many nuances in tone and hues in these broken ...rs as there are in the primary green.

...e method of preservation is as follows: mix one ...glycerine with two parts boiling water. Pour 2 or ...es of the solution into a narrow jar or tin or some ... vessel and stand the stem ends in it. Let them ...in until you can see that the solution has travelled ...through all the tiny veins in the leaves. At this ..., the texture usually changes becoming silkier and ...r. If the branches are allowed to remain in the ...ion too long they will sweat and the sticky exuda-...may fall on to the furniture. It is a simple matter to ...e when the leaves are sufficiently charged with the ...ion.

...ost flower shops sell certain imported foliage ...g the winter months and so long as these take ...r easily they can be preserved and stored for future ...nd used time and time again. To make sure that ...can be preserved, as soon as possible split the ...ends upwards for about 2 inches (this applies ...l branches deciduous and evergreen) and stand ...in 2–3 inches of hot water, at boiling point is best. ...he branches remain in this for several hours, over-...if possible. After this time you will be able to see ...n branches are not taking water, the leaves curl ...ook dry. These will not take the glycerine solution ...ugh it may be possible to use them dried. If you ...patience to press the individual leaves with a warm ...most foliage can be salvaged and used many times, ...ples are grevillea, oak, beech. Others can be opened ...t as possible and laid between newspaper and then ...r a heavy object, mattress or cushion for example. ...y blue gum or eucalyptus is, as its name suggests, ...antly grey-blue. There are roughly speaking two ...s which are marketed: the species and varieties with ...d penny-sized leaves and the long kind whose ...s are bent sickle-wise. Sometimes the latter kind ...be bought complete with lovely silver-grey buds ...coral-like tassel flowers. The buds will dry. These ...lyptus stems can be given just forty eight hours in ...olution and this period seems long enough to fix ...the form of the leaf and the colour. It is also ...ble to take eucalyptus from the preserving solution ...fferent intervals and so have the leaves in various ...s of hue. The longer these stay in, the darker the ...s become. Most subjects take more than four ...s.

...ost often people preserve those leaves which are ...ng colour in the autumn. To do this, one should ...ys cut or buy the branches long before the leaves ...n to fall.

Once the leaves are preserved they will last for years. They can be used entirely in dried flower and perpetuelle arrangements or they can be used from time to time with fresh flowers. Indeed, merely by preserving a few leaves you can have sufficient foliage to be able to furnish a vase with just a few flowers the year round and yet make good-sized decorations. If you preserve a little of several kinds you can frequently ring the changes. Store them away in some dry place in boxes or in plastic bags. If the stems have been stood in water, wipe them and make sure that they are dry before putting them in store.

As we have seen, a variety of any plant material makes flower arrangement easier and I would suggest that you try experimenting with various types of foliage to see which can be kept. If you buy gladioli or irises which have good entire healthy leaves, you might like to treat these. They turn a pleasant tan and they offer a contrast of shape.

You may also find that some of the leaves from house plants can be preserved – worth while doing if a plant, a cissus for instance, has grown too large.

Incidentally, certain leaves and infloresences, faded though they may be, are worth saving. Bromeliad blooms such as aechmea and vriesia look well in a large perpetuelle arrangement. Aspidistra leaves will last for years. You can curve these – and the gladioli

Left
Eucalyptus, stachys (lamb's tongues), rhodanthe and helichrysum with purple sea lavender (limonium or statice). Eucalyptus keeps its colour when dried. The large straw-daisies, helichrysum, are threaded on wire stems. Little rhodanthe flowers are bunched and then can be lengthened, tied to straws or mounted on wires.

Below
Grasses, honesty (lunaria), limonium and acroclinium. Lightweight vases should be one third filled with sand or shingle. The stemholder can be arranged on this. These stems are held in dry Oasis.

and iris leaves – by coiling them, tying them in place lightly with thread and then leaving them to soak overnight. They should then be dried thoroughly, after which they may be unloosened and pulled out to assume the necessary curves. Other leaves, such as shadow leaves, the name given to skeletonised magnolia and ficus leaves, and all those sold as magnolia can be given curves by coiling them round a candle or the handle of a wooden spoon.

Whether or not you wish to use only true flowers is a matter of personal taste. There are many manufactured flowers today. These are made from real plant parts but are not true flowers. They are attractive in their own way but generally speaking they are stiff in appearance so it is necessary to use plenty of informal material with them.

Look out for the bright orange Chinese lanterns or physalis, on sale in late autumn. During the summer buy small spikes of delphiniums and full spikes of annual larkspur and hang these upside down to dry in some warm, dry, dark place, an airing cupboard for instance. Buy grasses. Few of these on sale are in their natural state, they are either bleached or dyed, but if the dyed grass is of the colour most dominant in the arrangement you are planning it will not look too artificial. Slim pencil rushes keep for years and are a good buy. Most of these retain a bare portion of an inch or even much more above the flower portion. They look more attractive when this is cut away.

These attractive brown stems suit so many winter decorations and they look so right with tawny chrysanthemums, dried flowers of all kinds, fruits, berries and autumn and winter foliage.

One winter decoration which is very quick to do and most effective consists of five or seven pencil rushes,

the stems cut so that the 'flowers' are slightly fan These are impaled on the back portion of a pinho Shadow leaves or any large leaves, fresh, preserve pressed, are then arranged so that they too taper i one down to a fan on the left or right.

The tallest should reach to about halfway up stem of the tallest pencil rush. Those that need t tall are given false stems, usually the portion cut i the shortest pencil rushes. As a focal point you ca a large cone, or a gourd, surrounded by a sta flower grouping of smaller leaves. You can use fr of stipa grass to soften the outline.

False stems are easily applied and if you wan make the greatest use of many of the very decor short-stemmed subjects they are essential. Use str even drinking straws if you have no true tough gra thin twigs such as privet, lilac or even woody fl stems. Pipe cleaners are almost as useful as fl wires. These can be twisted round the short petio stem of any leaf. Where other types of false sten used, fasten the true stem to its mount with adh tape. Pine cones need false stems. Usually one ha encircle the cone near the base, pulling the wir cleaner right down so that it is wedged in the ba the scales. The ends of the wire stem are then t down under the cone and twisted round each o Cones make lovely wooden flowers and look well brown preserved foliage.

Various stem holders may be employed to hold materials. Since dried materials are usually very in weight they need anchoring in some way. Dry (is one of the best holders because one can insert the frailest stem without breaking it. This can als used in shallow containers in place of a pinho Oasis-Fix, a putty like adhesive will hold it firmly.

Below
Dried cardoons, delphiniums, onion seeds, squaw corn and hydrangea with a cabbage, apples, honesty and mahonia foliage. A cabbage makes a good focal point in both dried and fresh arrangements. The deeper the colour, the longer it will stay fresh. Leaf rosettes, either natural or assembled can be arranged in the same way as the cabbage.

Right
Larch branches and cones, physalis, sycamore keys, oak and mahonia leaves and grasses. Windfall branches from larch give height and the cones are flower-like. Pressed fallen leaves provide mass and colour. Some physalis can be cut open to expose the inner berries.

Home Decoration

Placing Plants

perhaps, this jungle light has much the same degree of intensity as does the light inside our homes. This explains why so many jungle plants make good house plants.

On the other hand, the popular flowering plants, mostly, have originated in sunny open climates and, as we have already seen, the more flowers a plant has the more light it needs when it grows indoors. Sometimes it is impossible to give it the amount of daylight it requires but there are methods of adjusting this, as we shall see.

The same conditions are required by any plant which has some colour other than green. All variegated foliage, leaves of two or more different colours, needs good light. However direct sunlight can cause more harm than good. The pretty scindapsus for instance, placed in strong sunlight will soon develop brown edges to its marbled leaves.

One might think that a windowsill is the natural place for any plant, especially after learning that a plant must have light, but one must realise that even windowsills receive different degrees or amounts of light according to what aspect they face. Fortunately, north, south, east or west-facing, we can find plants to suit any windowsill. Simply bear in mind that the sun pouring in early morning from the east will have nothing like the burning intensity of the sun shining in a south facing window midday or one which faces west on a late, hot, summer afternoon. North-facing windows tend to be both shady and cool and are ideal for many, indeed one might even say most plants, so long as the room itself is warm as well.

You can actually witness the influence of light upon growth. If you leave a plant undisturbed in a window it will, as you may know, gradually turn all its parts to

ou go out specially to buy a house plant, it is more likely that you already know exactly where you to place it. If someone gives you a plant, the case red because then you have to find a place in your for it. Light, the source of light, the quantity nt, the warmth of light, the aspect of light are all -tant to all plants.

ne of those which do not do well in our homes more than we can give them in the average house. which are adaptable and easy to grow find that tions in a home are not so very different from of their natural surroundings, even though the s of providing those conditions may differ con- bly.

ny of our popular leafy house plants grow natural- the shade of the jungle forests. They grow in ght but in the kind of daylight which is filtered through a ceiling layer of leaves. Surprisingly,

Previous pages
Columnea x banksii is a lovely and accommodating house plant which is too seldom seen. Its pretty trailing habit, with its masses of flowers, make it highly decorative. It likes lots of light but not direct sunlight.

Left
You can have plants in flower at all times of the year, even when snow falls thick outdoors! Here, *Euphorbia splendens* towers above an echeveria in bloom, bowls of mixed cactus and succulents and 'Peach Blossom' double early tulips. On the right is a yellow-flowering *Euphorbia splendens lutea*.

Below left
Facing a window in a corridor, *Hedera canariensis* has its roots in comparative shade, *Aechmea rhodocyanea*, tradescantia, croton (codiaeum), anthurium, a poinsettia (*Euphorbia pulcherrima*) which has flowered and the rarely seen *Scindapsus pictus* 'Argyraeus'.

Below
Ficus pandurata. The large, tough green leaves indicate that this fig should be grown in much the same way as the rubber plant. It needs slightly warmer conditions and care with watering.

he light, and leaves and flowers will show only undersurfaces when seen from the room. If you ‖ a plant to grow evenly, it is important to turn the ‖ a little each day, so that eventually all parts ‖ e the same amount of direct light.

can exploit this tendency. It is possible to grow a ‖ many leafy plants on walls which are opposite to a ‖ w or a glass door and these plants will become ‖ nely decorative because they will gradually turn ‖ leaves to face the window. This means that for ‖ people in the room itself, the plants show their ‖ aces.

rtunately, there are many plants which will grow ‖ his way, all the green, leaved climbers and creepers, ‖ stance. Remember, the greener, thicker, tougher ‖ af, the further back from the light the plant can ‖ wn. Bromeliads will also flourish here and if you ‖ inclined your wall can be decorated by a tree on ‖ a collection of the smaller types of these plants ‖ e fixed. Driftwood, or stripped clean tree branch, ‖ ces of cork bark made to look like a tree portion, ‖ e used as an anchorage. Alternatively, one can use ‖ d looking plastic mesh and fix the plants on this. ‖ some situations it is possible to grow variegated ‖ s this way, for instance, in a corridor or hallway ‖ e the opposite wall is not really very far from the ‖ w. Variegated ivies will roam prettily, especially ‖ rge-leaved *Hedra canariensis. Scindapsus aureus* ‖ ts varieties can be used for smaller effects. This ‖ little scrambler looks well planted at the foot of ‖ arge-leaved ivy. Mix it with the dark-leaved ‖ anthus which has purple undersides to its leaves ‖ ill provide contrast.

other position in which plants look attractive and ‖ , at the same time, they are in a more suitable ‖ on, is at right angles to a window. Here, according ‖ e size and style of a room, one can place a shelf, ‖ e, a large container, a group of plants stood on the ‖ or a trough.

en they are grouped this way you can often use ‖ r two plants to shield the rest from intense light. ‖ those which revel in it, a *Euphorbia splendens* or ‖ utsize cactus for example, near the glass and ‖ ate the rest so that those which prefer the shade ‖ rthest away from it.

you plan to use a trough under or in a window, ‖ few points in mind before you install it. Remember ‖ he plants will face outwards in time, if the trough ‖ the windowsill itself, or even if it is placed im- ‖ ately below it, unless you are prepared to turn the ‖ h every few days. It is possible to choose plants ‖ look very attractive with the light shining through ‖ Some of the ornamental begonias, and there are ‖ gh of these to give you variety, would be suitable ‖ is purpose and if you have a really warm room in ‖ r, *Iresine* 'brilliantissima' could be gorgeous. If ‖ grow climbers in the trough, and these can look ‖ tractive trained around, or in the case of an un- ‖ y view, on the window, remember that these do ‖ f their roots are not in full light. Either screen the ‖ of the climbers with bushy plants or stand the ‖ iner out of the light.

ose who know their subject talk of light levels, ‖ he levels of light influence plants in different ways. ‖ t has colour and although a detailed study of this ‖ t the subject of this book, we should say that the ‖ r of light affects a plant so much that it will ‖ me drawn or elongated or tight and compact ‖ rding to the kind of light under which it is grown. ‖ ight does not offer us many problems in this respect. ‖ w long light shines is another factor in growth, ‖ ll it the duration of light. This affects the develop-

ment of flowers so much that light duration is the basis of many horticultural methods used to produce flowers out of their natural season, such as poinsettias and all-year-round chrysanthemums. It affects us in the home in a simple way – we can use artificial light to prolong daylight and thus grow a greater range of plants.

Not all of us want to place plants in a window. In many homes there is not a suitable area in windows anyway and we have to place the plants in other areas about the home. Many of us feel that a corner, a dim hall or some other place could be enlivened if only some plants could be induced to grow there. But what really is the point of doing this if the plants cannot properly be seen? If they are lit some way, you ensure not only that the plants can be seen but also that they will be happier and will look more decorative simply because they will receive more light.

You will find that artificial light, even a reading lamp placed nearby and left switched on for four or five hours, greatly improves a plant's performance. If you have one which appears to have remained static for months, try putting a lamp near it and watch the new

rate of growth. Plants in living rooms often do so much better than plants which grow in rooms which are used only occasionally.

You can improve the light intensity in a room and at the same time direct a little more light on to a plant by a few simple means. Plants grow better where there are light painted walls than they do against dark backgrounds. A strategically placed mirror, or better still a wall covered by a mirror, will reflect light from a window or from some other source, on to a plant.

From these few observations, you will see that it is always a good plan to site your plants with an eye on the room's lighting as well as according to their own light requirements. Generally speaking, our reading lamps give off white light and although plants really have a preference for blue with red light (not to be confused with the colour of light bulbs) when these two colours are properly balanced, the ordinary home light is efficient enough for us to leave the complexities of light colours to the commercial grower. I use only ordinary lights in my own home and house plants grow happily in every room. If you have an understanding of lighting systems, you could possibly work plant wonders.

Many plants grow best if they are arranged at right angles to a window, with those which tolerate the strongest light placed nearest the glass. Here are ananas or pineapple, dracaena, chlorophytum, sansevieria, *Begonia masoniana* or the Iron Cross begonia, with the blue flowers of browallia nearby. *Begonia rex* hybrid, cyclamen, crotons (codiaeum) scindapsus and vriesia.

Opposite top right
Monsteras and bromeliads add colour and life to a kitchen which has enough space to accommodate them. The humidity and warmth of a kitchen (and even more of a bathroom) often make these rooms good situations for plants.

Opposite below
These plants are growing in a hall which has only one small window. However, white walls and a mirror placed strategically behind the plants reflect what little light there is and so help to increase light intensity.

This page
Monsteras are botanically philodendrons and like many others of this family they make handsome and distinctive climbers. They are most effective where they can be given space to display their attractive leaves.

Various forms of lighting can be used from 100 watt bulbs placed no further from plants than 4 feet and no nearer than 2, this is because the bulb generates heat and if placed too close the plants will become scorched; to strip and even spot lights. Fluorescent lighting provides cool light and thus eliminates the danger of scorching. Some plants, such as saintpaulias can be grown entirely under the influence of such lighting where it is not possible to provide daylight for them.

In another section we deal with plants in bottles or jungle jars, the term which covers all glass containers. Here I should mention that these gardens should never be stood in full sun, yet the plants must receive enough light or they will damp off and die. It is possible to provide them with both heat and light by converting the jungle jar into a lamp. You can buy fitments to fix into the neck of most of these glass containers and these will hold both the light bulb and lamp shade. The important thing here is that by such means the light is directed down on to the plants. As it is more ornamental than useful, the light is subdued and so cannot harm the plants.

Left
Rhoicissus capensis. Stron
growing climbers, especia
those belonging to the
grape-vine family, should
given plenty of room and
encouraged to climb. Giv
support they will soon co
wall. *R. capensis* is a stro
growing vine with woody
stems and leathery leaves
has attractive red fruit af
flowering.

Below and right
The leaves of plants natu
turn towards the most
important source of light
tendency which can often
used for decorative effect
The darker green and the
tougher the leaf, the furth
away from the direct sou
of daylight will a plant gr
Many climbers can be tra
along a wall opposite a
window.

Using the same principle, plants can be housed in a cupboard with glass doors, or in an alcove. The important thing is that the plants should never be grouped or grown with a light bulb close under them directing its dry warmth up to the plant's roots.

One of the kindest things plants can do is to bring life to a hearth no longer or seldom used for a real fire. The fireplace, so long as it is draught-proof, is an ideal place to grow plants. Here they can be watered and sprayed without harm. Many of the hearth and fireside accessories make attractive containers. One can, for example, pull out the ash pan under a fireplace, line it with strong plastic or a few layers of cooking foil and plant or plunge in this. Scuttles, coal boxes and hods, log baskets and large preserving pans and others can be filled with a variety of plants. If lighting can be installed the variety of plants can be greatly extended. However, even without this, there are plenty of plants which will thrive at this distance from windowlight, aspidistras, palms, syngoniums, philodendrons, spathiphyllums, bromeliads, sansevierias, for example.

Use plants to their greatest decorative advantage. If you are only just beginning to furnish a home, let them fill in the gaps meanwhile, you can always move them along when you have something more permanent. Let them act as screens, frames, furnishings. Let them mask a dreary scene, take attention away from an ugly or shabby corner. Use them to make a room look taller, wider, homelier and more welcoming.

Containers for them can be as varied as you wish, although it might be more pleasing if you search out only those which go with your general decorating theme. Make sure that the containers suit their setting and that they are deep enough to take the plants and

then set about making the plants look as though th... really were at home.

Certainly encourage climbers to climb and to do th... you will find that strong thread and drawing pins are... good guides as anything else, but remember also th... many climbers will also trail prettily. These look bes... they can hang down from a pedestal, shelf or torchè... Some, such as ivies, look well cascading from the b... of some very formal plants such as a *Ficus elastica* ... sansevieria.

Most strong-growing climbers such as cissus, rhoic... sus, ivy and several philodendron varieties can be train... to climb up in the corner of two walls and along the t... of the wall in one direction or another, or, if it suits y... right round the room. To support the plants, you ... stand a cane from the container to the ceiling or y... can tie one end of a thread to the short cane to wh... the plant is already attached. Take this up vertica... and pin it securely to the ceiling. Take more thr... along the top of the wall near the ceiling or in whate... direction or angle you prefer. The thread is inc... spicuous and really most effective. Obviously, it ne... to be strong, and nylon fishing line is ideal because t... will hold even weighty stems.

If you are going to use plants at high levels do ... member that warm air currents rise and that the pla... could suffer because of this. Those with lush grow... tips such as philodendrons are more likely to su... than say, rhoicissus. To prevent these from drying ... and so long as this does no damage to surroundin... spray the growing tips, and the rest of the plan... possible, with a little water, rain water preferably, fr... time to time. Use an atomiser and water at ro... temperature.

Grouping plants together successfully is not difficult and is never repetitive. Here, near a window framed by a rhoicissus are double tulips, a giant hippeastrum (so easy to grow), a striped vriesia in flower, crotons in a copper preserving pan and a stag horn fern or platycerium. The balance and shape of the group changes all the time as plants grow, flower and fade. It is fun to experiment and put together contrasting leaf shapes, textures and colours. Bulbs often look spectacular against plants grown principally for their foliage.

of *Tradescantia*
ris: 'Quicksilver', top
riegata, bottom left
urpusii is centre left
endula right; all these
ed good light if they
well coloured.
gs can be taken
m both plants and
ld be repotted each

ls like the shrimp
rican violets and
m to the left will
lly produce flowers.
n, cinerarias and
among others can be
om seed and timed to
winter.

Plant arrangements and dish gardens

In spite of the multitude of flowers on sale in our markets it is a fact that there are more kinds of plants, in other words, a greater variety, than there are cut flowers. Since this is so and since the plants themselves are such good value for money, why not use more of them in the same way that flowers are used, in arrangements about the house? True, a flower arrangement has its own special aura and beauty and can never be entirely replaced, but a plant arrangement will last

Far left
Pot grown eranthus or winter aconites, double tulips and yellow hyacinths arranged with chlorophytum in a shallow trug basket. Driftwood and moss hide and support the bulbs which are planted in potting compost.

much longer and changes shape as the plants grow.

It is one of the best ways of decorating centrally-heated homes for we can provide humidity for plants and so minimise the possibilities of adverse effects from the heat, but we cannot prevent fresh flowers from maturing and fading quickly.

We can make arrangements from foliage plants alone or they can be mixed with shorter-lived bulbous and flowering plants. They can also be grouped with cut flowers which can be refreshed from time to time as they fade and it is worth observing that flowers arranged with growing plants and sharing in the more humid micro-climate around them, do last a little longer than those which are grouped on their own.

Plant arrangements vary considerably, after all, even a trough planted with a number of different kinds or several of one sort, is a plant arrangement. However, we can make more imaginative and decorative arrangements than this.

One can use plants which are left in their pots and these can be plunged into various mediums, as we have already learned, or they can be simply packed round and wedged into position with damp moss or with one of the water-retentive foamed plastics, such as Oasis, which are used in flower arrangement. Alternatively, plants can be knocked from their pots and transplanted. Generally, we refer to the first method as arranging plants and to the second as making a dish garden but, as we shall see, the dividing line is not always absolutely clear cut. Sometimes we used both methods in one container.

We can also make arrangements with cuttings of all kinds, stem, leaf, offsets and stolons, in such a way that these will root in the water, although you can also arrange rooted cuttings, and they will go on growing so long as we remember to feed them with a weak soluble plant food from time to time. This is a simple and effective way of growing little plants and a good way of using any tips you may think it prudent to nip out from a vigorous mature plant. It is also an ideal way for a new indoor gardener to learn a little about propagating plants and growing generally.

The cuttings or plants are held in position by small stones or pebbles. Shingle is excellent for this purpose and is usually easy to find. Any water-tight container will do for this type of dish garden, known as a puddle pot, so long as it is deep enough to hold a good layer of pebbles. All manner of bowls and little bygones such as sauce boats, tureens, lidless teapots and large shells— so long as the water does not spill from these when you move the arrangement, and certain types of flower vases are vessels which can be used.

Generally speaking, the shallower the container the more securely you should anchor the plants.

If pebbles picked up from the seashore are to be used these should be well soaked and the water changed several times to remove the salt. Whenever pebbles and water are used to grow plants always lace them well with nuggets of charcoal to keep the water sweet.

Stem cuttings which will root in water include tradescantia, zebrina and any of this family; small leaved philodendron—unless you are to make a large puddle pot in which case some of the other larger-leaved kinds could be used; ivies, the small-leaved kinds look particularly attractive; syngonium and many other aeroids, plectranthus, peperomia, coleus, impatiens, rhoicissus, cissus, vitis, and even some outdoor annuals such as nasturtiums.

Chlorophytum offsets, especially if you select those whose roots are already well grown will soon begin to grow.

You can use small rooted plants, almost any kind if you do not mind them living but briefly. For more

Previous page left
If hyacinths are grown singly in pots, they can be arranged together or with other plant cuttings when in bud. Here there is a cutting of ivy roots in the same potting soil. Mos and driftwood cover the bulb themselves and the soil round them.

Previous page below
Aeroids are diverse in form and habit yet they blend well one with another. In the bow still in their pots, are variegate scindapsus and flowering anthuriums. Behind stand monstera and syngonium.

Left
Wickerwork and other non-waterproof containers can b lined with strong sheet plas or cooking foil to prevent t water from plants escaping and spoiling furniture. Her still in their pots, are arran a variegated hibiscus, *Maranta leuconeura* 'Erythrophylla', tradescant and fittonia—a collection o plants all with striking folia which complement each ot

Centre left
A piece of driftwood and r help to mask the pots in which these plants are still growing. The arum-like flo is the bloom of a spathiphyllum. Sansevieria and *Phoenix dactylifera*, th date palm, tower above *Hedera canariensis* on the and *H. helix* on the right v tufted chlorophytum at the centre.

Below left
Planted for a Mothering Sunday present this little b contains coloured primros a hyacinth, ivy and tradescantia. The two latte will go on growing in the bowl for a long time. The flowering plants should be removed when they have faded and be replaced wit fresh colour.

Right
A copper preserving pan comfortably holds pots of citrus, pilea 'Moon valley' *Calathea makoyana*, and tiny-leaved *Ficus pumila*. Moist peat fills the spaces between the pots and gen some humidity, which is necessary for the pilea and calathea in particular. All these plants should be sh from direct sunlight.

settled existence choose cyperus and carex, both swamp lovers. Wash the soil from roots before you arrange plants.

Although plants grown this way should be fed, they will never make such large specimens as they would if well grown in soil, but they do live for a long time. They are very dainty, with smaller leaves, more delicate trails and for this reason these little gardens give one the opportunity of using a greater variety of containers for plants than might be the case. And it follows, that this being so, one can use plant arrangements in more varied ways. For instance, such an arrangement in the right container can look delightful on a dressing table or on a desk. Puddle pots make good table centres, especially if you arrange some lovely glowing colour at the centre. This could be cuttings of coleus, some snippets or leaves from some bright-leaved begonia, or even, as a temporary measure, a little posy of fresh flowers. You could also grow or transplant some of the smaller bulb plants such as the pretty little Roman hyacinths which flower before Christmas, or crocus or any type of bulb which will grow well this way. Your choice will have to depend upon size because many of the forced bulbs are tall.

Many attractive flowers can be grown from bulbs planted in pebbles and water. This method seems to suit some narcissi particularly well but crocuses, hyacinths and, nowadays, even one variety of tulips, can be grown this way also. To make sure not only that you buy the correct types and varieties but also that you are kept up to date on new kinds, study a bulb merchant's catalogue and make your selection accordingly.

Any variety of narcissi recommended for indoor growing is almost certain to grow well in pebbles. The bunch-flowered or polyanthus varieties are said to do even better when grown this way than when grown in bulb fibre or soil indoors. Certainly I grow them successfully year after year.

To plant the bulbs, take a fairly deep bowl, the deeper the roots can go, the more securely will the bulbs be anchored, place a few nuggets of charcoal on the floor of the bowl and fill it to within 2 inches of the brim with the pebbles. Sit the bulbs on these, as close as you like so long as they do not touch. The noses of the bulbs should be well above the rim so adjust the level of the pebbles before you add water should this be necessary.

Right
Old fashioned double daffodils grow well in pots of soil. Tall 'Harvest Gold' are growing in fibre. Double tulips, scillas, grape hyacinths and hyacinths will all flower at the same time and can be complemented by cineraria.

Below
Like many other spring-flowering bulbs, crocuses can be grown in water anchored by stones or pebbles. A little charcoal keeps the water sweet. Crocuses are best kept in a cold place until the flower buds show when they can be brought into a warm room.

Above
Treat some plants as though they were flowers and make some beautiful decorations. Here the old ironstone tureen holds a matching cyclamen, a *Begonia masoniana* and cascading over the rim a *Plectranthus oertendahlii* with purple-backed leaves.

Left
Planted in good potting compost and growing happily together are *Ficus benjamina*, *Hedera canariensis*, with a vivid poinsettia and striking striped aphelandra before them, *Peperomia hederifolia* and *P. glabella* 'Variegata' with variegated leaves scrambling over the rim.

Right
A wonderful variety of textures, colours and forms can be brought together in a plant arrangement. Here at the centre is a croton or codiaeum, behind it are sansevieria, *Pittosporum undulatum,* and *Hedera canariensis*.
Tradescantia and vriesia are in front with *Hypocyrta glabra* on the left and aphelandra on the right.

More pebbles should now be arranged round and between the bulbs so that these are upright and well supported. Pour in water, clean rainwater if possible, so that its level is just under the surface of the pebbles. Place the bowls in a cool dark place until the roots are growing well. This is usually between five and eight weeks according to the type of bulb.

Bulb fibre is also an easy medium in which to grow bulbs and it suits many kinds including all of those which can be grown in pebbles. It should be used moist but not sodden and, once again, the noses of the bulbs should be above the surface after planting.

The critical time for spring-flowering bulbs grown indoors is immediately after planting. The essential factor is that the bowls or other containers should be stored in a cold, dark place until the roots are well formed and the shoots are actually growing out from the bulbs. They can then be brought indoors. This is best done in stages, first into a cool place for a few days, and then into a warmer one and so on. If the bulbs are not treated this way you might find that the flowers are stunted, malformed or unattractive in some other way.

After trying many methods of cool, dark, storage including traditional plunging of bowls out of doors, I have found that the simplest and most effective way is to wrap each bowl inside a black plastic bag and to stand this in the coldest place you have—not the freezer though. I keep mine on the north wall of the garage, indoors. I have kept them outdoors on north-facing windowsills and roof areas, on a cold landing of an outer staircase to a flat and in a cellar. Any of these places will do.

As I said earlier, bring the bowls into the warmth and light gradually and once you have them in a window, give them a quarter turn each day to keep them growing evenly.

Whether you force your own bulbs or buy them ready grown be sure to water them, but once they are in bloom give them very little or they will mature too quickly. Always water the soil around the bulbs and try not to pour water over the bulbs themselves. When you spray your other plants to freshen them, give bulb flowers a little shower as well. They will keep fresher longer.

It is not really a good plan to grow mixtures of bulbs, although it is pleasant to make arrangements of different kinds if these are mature together. As you would expect, bulbs can be easily fitted into all manner of plant arrangements, in or ex-pot. You can plan a bulb and plant arrangement well ahead if when you plant a bowl with bulbs in fibre you also plant one or more empty flower pots. When the bulbs are brought into the warm room, you can then remove the empty pot and replace it with a full one. This could be another type of bulb flower, perhaps for instance, crocuses with narcissi, or it could be a flowering plant, a cyclamen, or a leafy plant or two.

If the bulbs are growing in pebbles and water you can introduce any of the puddle pot cuttings. If you do not mind being extravagant, you can wash the roots of an anthurium and plant it among the pebbles because this plant will grow happily this way. It will thrive also alone in a hyacinth glass.

To prevent them from becoming spoiled, metal and wooden containers can be lined. Quite often a strong waterproof plastic bag will do—you can cut it or roll it down so that it fits the container and is inconspicuous. Cooking foil offers extra lining and so far as wooden containers are used indoors, if these are precious and not simply plant troughs, it is wise to use foil and plastic.

Incidentally, speaking of plastic bags, those black sleeves, sold as substitutes for flower pots, are often much easier to fit into containers than the rigid pots. If you are building up a stock of small plants for plant arrangements you might care to bear this in mind.

Sometimes a shallow container can be given extra height and so made suitable for a plant with a deep root ball by lining it with foil or plastic and raising it at the back. This subterfuge will be hidden by plants arranged in the foreground. You can also retain the soil by using pieces of cork bark, driftwood and flat shells inside the rim.

The pleasant thing about using plants with flowers, or about grouping flowering plants, is that many containers one might pass over if one were looking for a container for a single plant, or for a collection of green plants, prove to be perfect when flowers are introduced. Old wash basins, which are often highly patterned, are ideal especially in cottage interiors. They are deep enough at the centre to take a large pot with a tall plant yet shallow enough at the edges to take the small pots in which hedera (ivy), tradescantia, plectranthus and other scramblers are often grown and wide enough to allow one to build up a really good collection.

As I said earlier, the dividing line between a plant arrangement and a dish garden is not always clear cut, and using a wash basin could offer an example of this, for I would suggest that where the area near the rim is too shallow to take a small pot comfortably, it might be more convenient and effective to add soil at this point and to plant the scramblers. Alternately, strike cuttings of them and let them root here to be moved later when the arrangement is dismantled.

The types of containers which can be used are legion. They include large soup tureens, coal scuttles, preserving pans, log baskets, urns, pitchers, to mention only a few.

Obviously, one has to be guided by size for a large container filled with potted plants can be very heavy and difficult to move around. One can lessen weight by filling a deep container to the required depth with foamed plastic. The pots can be pressed into this and they will be held at whatever angle is required. A further advantage is that the plastic stays nicely moist, or will do so if it is watered from time to time, and thus will generate a pleasant humid area immediately around the plant. Just one word of warning, plants find this substance so agreeable that after a time they grow down into it, so if you think it time the plants were repotted, examine the pot bottoms from time to time.

Left
Colchicum autumnale (ofte wrongly known as the aut crocus). Flowers will grow this bulb without the assist of soil or water and in a v short time. Simply stand t bulb in some vessel or saucer to anchor it. After flowering, plant the bulb i the garden where it will produce its leaves in sprin and flower again the follo autumn.

Right
Plants need not be transpla when they are arranged. A these—dracaena, coccolob anthurium, cryptanthus a scindapsus are in their individual pots, some of w are raised and hidden by t plants before them. Cocco is a plant that will grow v tall and ideally needs spac to display its boldly shape leathery leaves. Very your plants are an attractive addition to an arrangeme

From my own point of view I find tall or pedestal flower vases to be some of the best containers for displaying house plants. Grouped in these, the plants are lifted well above the level of whatever surface on which the arrangement is to stand. They give elegance to arrangements, especially when trailing plants can be allowed to cascade down over the edge for some inches. There is another point to be borne in mind. When you have to move the arrangement you can do so easily and without disturbing the plants in any way, simply by holding a portion of the pedestal.

While bulb bowls are not in use they can hold plant arrangements and, of course, not all of these need be large, often three or four small plants look quite attractive especially if the container is a little out of the ordinary. If you have a choice, bear in mind that a container with sides that slope so that its mouth is much wider than its base gives you a good area of soil surface on which the plants can display themselves. If the container is deep, 4 inches at least, there is room for some roots near the base to reach down to the bottom and for others to be spread out nearer the surface.

redients for a puddle pot
simple: gravel, water and
w nuggets of charcoal to
it sweet, an attractive
ainer and a selection of
se plant cuttings. Arrange
cuttings as you would a
, with trailers over the
of the container and an
resting focal point in the
re—a coleus shoot in this
. Strip the stem ends of
s before anchoring them
ace with some of the
gle or whatever other
s are used. Finally, top
ith water and feed the
ts from time to time.

As the containers you will use have no drainage hole it is necessary instead to install a layer of what is termed drainage material on the floor of the vessel. This provides essential air spaces into which water will be rapidly sucked when the plants are watered. One of the best drainage layers and certainly one of the most simple to provide today is made of small nuggets of charcoal. At one time broken flower pot crocks were recommended but these are becoming rarer and rarer. Stones and shingle may also be used but they tend to make the bowl very heavy.

The first rule for a successful dish garden is to provide good soil. Although the plants will retain their pot soil or root balls, more soil will be needed to pack round them. Do not use soil dug up from the garden or countryside for this may contain harmful pests and fungi. Buy a bag of good potting compost. This is on sale in garden shops and chain stores. Buy small amounts unless you are making many dish gardens because the soil mixture deteriorates during storage.

Before deciding which container you are going to use, examine your plants. The depth at which they should be planted is determined by their crowns, the part of the plant at the junction of root and top. The crown should never be further above or below the new soil level than it was originally.

In the finished arrangement, the soil surface do have to be level, indeed it is usually better if it so. Raise it either in the centre or to one side. A soil area gives a plant greater depth for its roots. have plants from varied sizes of pots you can those from the largest pots in the raised soil are this point also, place those plants which like to b drained, sansevierias, peperomias, succulents bromeliads.

Having decided what plants you intend to together, water them and let them drain well befo begin, that is, unless they have been very re watered. Knock them from their pots one at a ti you proceed so that their roots are not exposed air any longer than is necessary. Before you begi a good plan to arrange the plants on the table in ro the pattern you intend to follow. You will then b to see what placement is really practical and whe tallest or shortest plants ought to go.

Spread a layer of soil over the drainage layer. D make this too deep or you may have difficulty comodating the plants. As you arrange their roc the soil, determine whether and where the soil raising. Try to disturb the roots as little as pos

Below
Sedum sieboldii. A plant that will withstand quite cool conditions and because of its semi-succulent nature can be left for several weeks without water. It dies down in winter.

plants should stand upright but if you want some
tail over the rim of the container or to lean away
the centre, tilt them and slip some soil under them
edge them in place. At the end, see that all the roots
covered with soil. Press this down firmly so that the
t is as solidly anchored as if it has been growing
way always. However, guard against panning the
ce, that is making it so hard that water cannot pass
ugh it easily. If it flows off, the surface is too hard.
ake sure that you have left room for watering. The
evel should be at least a ½ inch below the rim, even
ises in the centre.
nally, water the plants carefully, preferably by
ying the leaves and the soil surface. It is important
the soil is not made sodden. Stand the arrangement
place so long as this is not in a very sunny spot.
after some time, during which the plants have
n well and spread over the surface, you find it
ult to water the bowl it may be best to lower the
e arrangement gently into a sink filled with water or
some other larger vessel. Hold it there until the
bles stop rising to the surface, then allow the
lus water to drain away. Cacti often need this
iod of watering but remember not to do this more
once a month in winter.

It is not wise to mix cacti with other kinds of house
plants. Fortunately, these make charming arrangements when grown together and you can find sufficient
variety among them to make contrasts of shapes and
textures. Some succulents go well with them, especially
those with bloom on their leaves or those which
flower well such as rocheas and crassulas. Sansevierias
can be grown with cacti.

Some succulents can be mixed with the majority of
the other house plants you are likely to use in arrangements. Again, rochea and crassulas and *Sedum sieboldii*
'Medio-variegatum' is a prettily variegated plant.
Although it dies down in winter it is well worth
collecting.

Whether you make a plant arrangement or a dish
garden, aim for contrasts. Most groups look their
prettiest with a plant or two scrambling over the edge of
the container. In the central zones plant rosettes or
distinctive broad-leaved plants such as the beautifully
marked *Begonia Rex* varieties, calathea, maranta,
pilea and some bromeliads. For height and grace there
are palms, sansevieria, *Fatsia elegantissima*, ivies
trained vertically, dracaenas especially the prettily
coloured *Dracaena marginata* and the green and white
striped *D. sanderiana*. There are many more.

Below
Most kinds of cacti and
succulents will grow well and
last for years in a shallow dish
garden. In this one a small
juniper has been added as a
temporary contrast, since it
will have to be removed and
transplanted later.

Bottle gardens

Bottle gardens or jungle jars as they are sometimes called are extremely decorative and even appealing but apart from these qualitites they can also play a useful role. In them it is possible to grow many plants which cannot be expected to do so well outside the glass walls, in rooms where the atmosphere is dry and the temperature sometimes fluctuates. Of course, it is possible also to grow similar plants within the glass as are on the outside, but if a bottle garden offers you the choice of

Left
A specially designed case with a regulator for ventilation, placed on a deep drip tray, provides a perfect atmosphere for plants and enables one to grow some of the more temperamental kinds, even when the arrangement is stood in a warm, dry place.

Below
A large brandy glass-type container makes an attractive jungle jar and is easy to fill. Almost any deep glass will serve the same purpose even if it is slightly colour tinted. Jungle jars seldom need watering. In this one are selaginella, fern, *Begonia rex* and carex.

adding to your collection of house plants, why not take it and have a new arrangement to place as well?

Some of the more choosy plants you can expect to grow – and can buy – are species of selaginella which are mossy and fern-like and carpeting; *Nertera depressa*, another carpeting plant with tiny leaves and little orange berries, many kinds of the tender ferns such as the wiry-stemmed maidenhairs, miniature tender palms, crotons, fittonia, calathea, maranta, peperomia, pellaea, pilea and pellionia.

Some of these you will recognise as being good room plants under certain conditions and the important thing about using these in bottle gardens is that they are fairly slow growing. They also provide colour and texture contrast. It is possible to fill a bottle with just one type of plant, say a colony of bromeliads or ferns, but usually they look more attractive when the plants are mixed.

Unless you know your plants well, do not be led into thinking that if a plant is small and has small leaves it is bound to be suitable for this type of garden. Helxine now known botanically as *Soleirolia soleirolii*, sometimes called baby's tears, has the tiniest leaves yet it would soon take over the entire bottle. The same applies to the creeping ficus, to tradescantia and zebrina. Of course, if you find that a plant is growing too rapidly you can always take it out and pot it in the usual manner and grow it elsewhere. If you have a bottle garden for several years, this becomes necessary.

Jungle jars have become so popular that today special glass containers are being produced for this purpose. Unlike the old-fashioned glass carboys these are made with necks large enough to allow an arm to reach down inside. Another and easy-to-fill jungle jar is an outsize brandy balloon type glass. Storage jars and even wine and cider jars and bottles can be used, so long as it is possible to plant them.

The glass is usually clear but it can be tinted, light brown, light blue and green. The important thing is that it shall be clean and kept clean.

If the neck of the glass is large enough for you to insert your hand, planting will offer few problems but when you are filling a jar which has a narrow neck you should be both careful and patient.

First group the plants in the way you hope to see them in the jar. I suggest that you slope the soil, so keep this in mind, remembering that this will heighten any plant you set at the top of the slope.

If you cannot insert your hand you will need to improvise a tool or two so that you can make a hole for the plant, guide the plant into the hole, cover it and firm the soil round the plant afterwards. Often one thick stick will do the lot but more often it is helpful to lash a kitchen spoon to a cane to use to dig out holes. An old-fashioned wooden cotton reel on the end of a cane will make a neat little rammer with which you will be able to pat the soil round the plants. These should always be set firmly in the soil otherwise their roots will not be able to absorb nourishment and they may sicken and die.

As with all containers, troughs, large bowls, dish gardens, a drainage layer is essential. The safest thing to throw or pour in is charcoal which is so light in weight that it cannot crack the glass. If you use small pebbles such as pea gravel, do not pour this straight into the jar on to the glass base, but first pour in a thin layer of peat to cushion the impact of the stones.

To fill a carboy, make a funnel or cylindrical chute of strong paper or card. Insert one end of this into the neck of the jar. First pour in the peat, then the gravel and lastly the soil.

This drainage layer needs to be quite deep, 2 inches

Top
Planting a bottle garden. Make sure that the inside of the glass is sparkling clean before you begin work. Strew a few nuggets of charcoal on the floor of the container before adding some sand for drainage.

Slope the soil slightly. This is easily done if you put the lowest plant in first near the front, cover its roots with soil and put the next plant in position. Be sure to secure the roots of each plant and at the

end gently ram the surface to firm it.

The little cryptanthus has been tied to a mossy branch and arranged out of the soil. The selaginella and tiny fern will carpet the soil, while the shrubby variegated euonymus and carex rush will provide contrast of shape and colour. Selaginella has small, scale-like leaves like a tiny fern and the species that are low growing and creeping are ideally suited to the cool humidity of a bottle garden.

or so for a large carboy and proportionately less for smaller jars.

Soil composts should not be too rich or the plants will grow too fast. The best medium is John Innes Potting Compost No. 2. The amount of soil you use will depend upon the size of the container; you should be able to see more glass and plants than soil but it is the depth of the plants' roots which should guide you. These must be properly planted.

To get the soil in the right condition so far as moisture is concerned, calculate how much you need, take about one third of this amount and spread this out on newspaper to dry. Spray the other two thirds until it is just moist, uniformly so, and when you take a handful and squeeze it gently it should just cling together.

This dampened compost should go in first. The dry compost follows to form a top dry layer which should help to seal in the moisture.

As with dish gardens, water the plants beforehand and allow them to drain thoroughly. Knock them from their pots in turn. If the aperture of the glass is very small it may be necessary to shake off any loose soil from the roots so that the plant can be slipped in easily. The leafy portion is no problem because this naturally contracts as it is pushed root first through the opening. To make sure of this, hold the plant by the tips of its leaves, or if it is tall, gather its branches or leaves up near its centre stem, so that this top portion is made really slim. Make a hole in the soil, tilt the jar and aim for the hole. This actually, is easier than it sounds. Direct the plant into the hole with the stick or with the spoon. Make the hole for the next plant directing the soil round the roots of the first plant. Ram the soil down before tilting the jar for the second time. Continue this way until all the plants are in position.

Inevitably, some soil particles will dirty the inside of the jar. It is not wise to spray these off with water, which seems the natural thing to do because the soil will be made too moist. A feather duster fixed to a strong piece of wire, which can be bent as required, is the easiest way to clean the glass. If the plants' leaves have soil on them, lash a fine paint brush to a cane and clean them.

If the soil is properly moist the plants should settle in and you should not need to water it for some weeks. If the balance is right you should see a little condensation or dew on the interior each morning. However, if this seems excessive—so much that there are several runnels and large drops on the glass, there is too much moisture in the soil and it would be prudent to remove the moisture from the glass to prevent it running back into the soil. Lash a tissue to the end of a wire or the bow of a coat-hanger to do this. When the time comes that you see no condensation, this is an indication that the soil needs watering. To do this, gently spray the interior glass. This will help to clean it at the same time. Do not feed the soil or the plants will grow too well.

Combining plants and flowers

...ce you enjoy arranging plants you will not find it a ...at step to use cut flowers with them nor to add to ...se two all the accessories and lovely natural materials ...ich are associated with flower arrangements.

...You might begin, as I did, from a purely practical ...d. If a bowl of mixed plants looks a little spent and ...ds brightening, what could be easier or more ...tantly effective than to push some kind of water ...sel into the soil, among the plants and hidden by ...m, and then to fill it with a few fresh flowers? You ...d so few and yet the result is often quite remarkable. ...rom such a simple beginning, you will find that ...-et-fleur, as such arrangements are called, offers ...a most interesting and exciting way of decorating ...r home. In the first place, you will never be at a ...s for basic colours because the plants will provide ...se. All you have to do is to find the few flowers that ...required.

...s you would expect, those which grow on plants ...n to some of our house plants always look good in ...-et-fleur. These are such flowers as anthuriums, ...ns, cyclamen, which though they may seem a little ...ensive at times should last well. Orchids, also ...emely long lasting, look delightful with house plants ...lo any of the smooth-stemmed bulb flowers; in ...ng, narcissi which include daffodils, freesias, tulips, ...later in the year, gladioli, lilies, nerines, *Amaryllis ...donna* (the outdoor plant) and the late-flowering ...zostylis.

...Many shrubs' blossom looks good, especially in ...ter or early spring; magnolias, azaleas and rhodo- ...drons, taken from their usual environment and set ...ng exotic house plants have an extremely rich and ...derful effect.

...enerally speaking leafy subjects look too fussy and ...ese are to be used it is usually best to remove most ...heir own foliage so that the house plants take the ...light. Examples are roses, paeonies, dahlias.

...the same way, soft petalled flowers may not show ...s well as you had hoped, anemones and chrysanthe- ...ns, for instance.

...ou can often use a few flowers to emphasise a ...ain feature of a plant's foliage, colour for instance. ...n the underside of a leaf may be vividly coloured ...yet, because of all the greens which surround it, ...may not be very noticeable. Choose some flower ...ch matches this colour and make a pot-et-fleur and ...will see a great difference. Study the plants' ...urs before you go to shop for the flowers. You will ...colours other than greens in stems, stipules, bracts ...tendrils.

...se flowers also to accentuate shapes. Irises are ...ctive when arranged with tall spiky sansevieria ...ibly because this pot plant's leaves are similar in ...e to iris leaves. Arrange pointed gladioli with low

growing large leaves such as begonias. Arrange posies of violets, pansies and tiny cyclamen with little ivies. Use vivid tulips with a vivid cordyline.

Pot-et-fleur can incorporate planted bowls or you can let the plants stay in their pots and arrange them individually. Just the same rules apply as for plant arrangements; you will need suitable containers, a drainage layer and good soil if you are planting the bowl, and plenty of wedging and plunging material if you are arranging plants. If you raise many plants yourself, pot some of these in the black plastic sleeve-type flower pots. As I said elsewhere, you will find these so much more easy to squash into a container than rigid flower pots.

You will need plenty of material for masking and hiding pots and the vessels you use to hold the flowers. The latter can be arranged in many ways. When you fill a bowl you can plant a few empty vessels, deep cream cartons, cigar tubes, small glass or plastic tablet tubes, pointed metal cones which you can buy at the florists' and the plants' roots can find their way round these. You will not then disturb them when you remove the water containers to clean them—flowers die quickly if containers are allowed to become soiled. Keep them as clean as dishes and cutlery. You can also use blocks of foamed plastic inside a small piece of plastic sheeting, this makes it easier to lift out the plastic if you should wish to replace it. After you have made one or two pot-et-fleur arrangements you will soon grasp the essentials.

Of course, many of the plants will hide all the mechanics of the arrangement, but sometimes you will find that a pot rim still shows or the top of a tablet tube appears above plant level. Driftwood, cork bark, coral, sea-fan and sea-shells and dried fungi of many kinds, especially the large bracket-fungi, are some of the accessories you can introduce into pot-et-fleur so that they form part of the design and serve a more useful purpose at the same time.

Do not hesitate either to mix dried materials with your growing plants and fresh flowers. After all, this is nature's way. Dried lotus lily seed heads look extremely lovely used alone or clustered as the focal point surrounded by lively leaves; cocoa palm boats or husks can be arranged with plants other than palms and these will hold flowers, fresh or dried if you wish; so-called dessert-spoons, really the dried ends of agave leaves sometimes sold varnished, will add height and a certain strangeness to familiar plants; skeletonised leaves can be used to back and to throw into contrast those of a more substantial nature.

There really is no limit to the ways you can use flowers and plants to decorate your home.

Far left
Regal lilies, dracaena, *Begonia rex,* blue coco beans, camphor pods, cherries and driftwood. Containers with wide tops are best for plant and flower arrangements. There should be space for small flower pots as well as for vessels for the flowers. All can be effectively hidden.

Left
Tulips and scented pelargonium, ivy and garden arum leaves, *Begonia rex* plant and fruit. Plants, flowers and fruit can be grouped together in many ways to make unusual and highly decorative arrangements.

Above
A bowl of growing plants a
cut flowers arranged togeth
originally made as a gift.
Saintpaulia and crocuses ar
combined with cut stems of
catkins, heather and snowd
all placed in a kitchen bowl.
Other plants could be adde
quickly and without troubl
when the cut flowers have
to make a lasting plant
arrangement.

Below left
Wayside grasses, *Hedera
canariensis*, and gloxinia.
small flower arrangements
and pot plants are concent
in one area their decorative
value is often greater than i
they are dispersed. Grasses
are long lasting and can be
left to dry in situ.

Right
The growing plants framin
carnations are sansevieria,
Hedera helix 'Glacier' and
the left is the pretty marbl
scindapsus and opposite t
yellow blotched sedum. C
sprigs of the silvery senecio
hide pots and flower contai

Harmonising plant and flower colours

In the previous chapter I said that you can often use a few flowers to emphasise some colour in a plant's foliage, and the more you combine and arrange plants and flowers the more you will appreciate the importance of colour harmony.

A simple green plant is likely to suit any setting and if it goes in a green outer pot it will merge discreetly enough with its surroundings. However, you could get much more value from it than that.

Although at first glance they may seem to be so, few leafy plants are in one colour. Even those described as 'green' are unlikely to be produced in one plain definable colour. Such a plant is much more likely to hold many hues of green. It may have tints in its young shoots which are so light and delicate that they seem to offer contrast to the old leaves. Other parts of the same plant may be in deep tones or shades. Often in the oldest leaves there may be a different green on the upperside than there is on the underside. Leaf stipules, tendrils, aerial roots, flowers like those of some of the aeroids, and fruits will extend the variety of hues within this main colour.

Green is a secondary colour of the spectrum, made of a mixture of yellow and blue. In a mixture of plants we can always find some which are more yellow than green and others may have so much blue in them as to be described as glaucous. They all look well together because they are linked by a common colour. Together they make an analogous harmony.

This variation of hue is fascinating and any plant owner will find great enjoyment in discovering just how much variation of one colour exists in one leaf. But there is more to it than that. Many plants, like flowers, have natural colour contrasts and harmonies. Take as a simple example the familiar green rubber plant *Ficus elastica decora*. Often in this plant, perhaps only at certain stages of its growth or times of the year, we can find traces of the most beautiful carmines and magentas. The growing tip may be covered with a vividly coloured sheath. A hue of the same colour, or perhaps a shade, might also be found in the stems or in the raised veins on the underside of the leaf. Many green leaves have beautifully coloured undersides: cinerarias, cyclamen and saintpaulias are familiar examples. Conversely, highly coloured or patterned foliage, begonias for instance, often has plain undersides.

The study of colour is truly fascinating and the purpose of these brief remarks is to suggest that by taking more interest in plant colours we can get greater value from their decorative role in our homes.

Let us refer back to the few simple examples given. It could be that in a furnishing scheme the carmine we see in a rubber plant (incidentally, a natural complementary colour harmony) could give you a lead on what other colours to use in the room where it stands.

Flowering plants in those colours placed near it are likely to have a greater impact and give more pleasure than others. The same applies to flower arrangements, in which, of course, greens can also be blended. Depending on your requirements, containers, some ornaments, pictures, even soft furnishings could follow this guidance.

However, as one can see by the illustrations in this book, plant colour covers the spectrum. Some people have a natural flair for colour, but those who find it difficult to harmonise one colour with another can be helped by the plants and flowers themselves.

If you love plants, then you are bound to admire leaves. As we have already learned, arrangements of different kinds of plants can look very attractive, even when they do not share a flower between them. In a plant arrangement no one colour ever seems to fight or clash with another (although some associations are more exciting than others, as one would expect) and perhaps this is because there is between them the bond of sap–all green brothers under the skin!

The same is true of flowers, but before we deal a little more freely with floral colour harmony I should like to suggest that you experiment with 'flower' arrangements from leaves rather than from cut blooms. A leafy table centre, for instance, is always a good idea. You can keep the arrangement low in stature but very

varied in nature and you can also keep it ever-changing, for it is so easy to take out a faded leaf and slip in some new discovery.

There is no reason why these leaves should be picked from your beloved house plants, although on the other hand there are times when these can be usefully employed. A cyclamen, for instance, which has finished blooming and is beginning to die down is likely to have enough good leaves for you to gather three or four if and when you need them. A rhoicissus, ivy, philodendron, chlorophytum or any plant which is growing just a little too vigorously for your convenience can be pruned from time to time, and there is always the advantage that these prunings can later be treated as cuttings. Indeed, some may even begin to root in water while they are part of the newly created arrangement. This is also often the case with begonia leaves.

[Partial left-margin text, captions]

ined stem holders, in this
ire-netting impaled on
older, facilitate
ement when stems of
g thicknesses and
ials of different weight
ed. Tall stems go down
h the netting onto the
nts. The brilliant focal
provided by the berries
lanced by the solid reds
llows of the dahlias
rysanthemums.

st a background of green
, ivy and gladiolus leaves,
ated kale with matching
, cupressus and a golden
make the contrasting
ony. Grey green lichen
ats provide height and a
st of textures.

wing page left
me vase that is pictured
lays a different role, its
e pattern lines guiding the
of the arrangement. Drift-
iris seed pods, fresh and
kale leaves, laurel,
ngeas, dried artichokes
matoes mounted on a
stem, are simple materials
ok distinctive.

Right
The yellow crinkly leaves
cut from stems of forced
rhubarb. An arrangement
this uses freshly bought o
picked daffodil buds with
blooms. As these fade, ne
ones can be bought and t
roles reversed.

Far right
Simple complementary co
harmony, orange and blue.
by studying the dahlias and
using them as a guide we
elaborate and create a mo
subtle colour scheme. The
ligularia leaves and the
interior of the dish repeat
tones in the dahlias' centre

Below
A combination of preserv
beech leaves, pussy willow
dogwood stems with fresh
variegated kale, wild ivy t
and cuttings from house p
which include variegated i
and cordyline leaves.

Other leaves are easy to find, even if you have no garden. Preserved leaves can be used with fresh foliage. Fallen leaves can be pressed and fern fronds treated in ways I have suggested elsewhere. Certain everyday leaves that one does not usually consider as material for flower arrangement can be used, for example, cabbage, parsley, forced rhubarb, beetroot and carrot. Instead of a flower or a flower cluster at the focal point of an arrangement you can use the thick rosettes from any attractive succulent plant.

Some people find great satisfaction in making monochromatic arrangements, in which all kinds of green plant materials play a role. These may include lichened branches, green berries, seed heads, catkins, stems and buds, and as one would expect, green flowers. Actually there are many green flowers, some of them so lowly and inconspicuous that we tend to pass them by unseen. On the other hand, some are so handsome that keen flower arrangers seek them out. Hellebores and spurges are favourites. Grasses also are green flowers. All of these help us to make arrangements full of interest.

Probably one sees more monochromatic arrangements in green than in any other colour because there are so many green plants to be found, but this should not limit you. You can also try to make yellow, blue, brown, orange, carmine or any other colour leaf ensembles. Better still, mix them and see just how vivid and varied you can make a non-flower arrangement.

Once you have experimented with leafy materials alone you may find it helpful to bring in other accessories. Fruits seem a natural addition. Quite often you can arrange these in a temporary decoration, for a dinner party table for instance, and then use the ingredients for a more practical purpose while they are still at their best. However, there are many other fruits than those you buy to eat, hedgerow and garden berries among them, and there are also many attractive vegetables.

As I have already referred to secondary colours, perhaps it would be helpful to give a few more facts, which should help the arranger to create attractive colour harmonies. The colours of flowers and plants are those of the rainbow, in which there are the three primary colours, red, yellow and blue. From these are derived the secondary colours. If you look at a rainbow you will see how naturally these are made. Blue overlaps with yellow to make green; yellow with red to give orange; and if we could bring the two outer edges together as we do when we make an artificial colour wheel, to make its two edges touch, we should see that when the red and blue meet they make purple.

These, then, are the true spectral colours but, as you know, in plant life and elsewhere colours vary considerably. Just think of the number of reds there are, for instance. Some colours are much more definite than we see in the rainbow through strong light. We say that such colours have a rich or strong tone. When colours have a degree of grey or even black in them we call them shades and, as I said earlier, when the colours are thin, i.e. when they contain much light, we say that they are tints. Then there are all the variations which lie between the true colours, the hues, to which we often give descriptive names, such as jade green, turquoise blue, ruby red, primrose yellow, lavender blue and salmon pink.

Each primary spectral colour has its natural opposed secondary colour which is known as its complementary. Thus orange is complementary to blue, green to red and purple to yellow. You can never create a discord if you put two complementaries together. Think how good a green plant looks inside a red pot.

Sometimes the two spectral complementaries are a

little too strong for some people's taste when used in flower arrangement. They may prefer to reduce one or both colours to a paler tint. In some settings, for example, a green plant might look better in a pink pot than in a scarlet one. Soft apricot flowers might suit a blue room better than bright orange ones and violet delphiniums be more pleasing against pale lemon walls than against buttercup yellow. Don't imagine though that it is necessary to have equal quantities of complementary colour.

Dealing with flowers and plants differs from handling fabrics and paints because, as we have seen, there is certain to be some other colour or hue present, usually green or some hue of it. So when we are making harmonies we always have to compromise and take this extra colour into account. Actually this can be very useful. Green makes a wonderful buffer between one vivid colour and another. Anyone who is undecided can always select a green container and be almost certain of choosing a harmonious colour for its contents. Of course the green of the vessel could exactly match some green in the plants or flowers and then the harmony would be even more pleasing. It is also safe to take tints to their limit, which of course is white, and shades to theirs, which is black. This means that flowers and plants look right in white or black containers.

There are some other safe colours also. When complementaries are mixed together they make what are known as 'broken' colours. These are pleasing, safe, familiar, almost neutral colours, the natural ones of leaf, bark, branch and stone. Orange and blue make a grey, green and red make a brown, and yellow and purple make a tan. You can often see a natural example of the last in a pansy flower, where you will sometimes see yellow and purple and tan all together. Of course these broken colours will vary according to the quantities of one or other colour in them. Take some water paints and mix them yourself to see what results you get.

So far as flower arrangements are concerned, not everyone likes to see contrasts, even if complementary and therefore harmonious. Many people like to see a more subtle blending of hues. As I have already said, monochromatic arrangements are extremely popular and there is no doubt in my mind that, among these, all-white flower arrangements come highest in popularity, but of course this is a matter of personal taste. Whatever your favourite colour, it really is a fascinating pastime to set about making an arrangement which plays on the colour keyboard from its low shades, through the rich tones and up to the palest tints.

An analogous popular colour harmony is that which uses the neighbouring colours on the spectrum. Thus we can have arrangements in which the flowers go from blue, red to purple; from yellow, orange to red; from yellow, green to blue; but with all the nuances of tints, shades and hues. Many familiar flowers naturally produce blooms in analogous harmony.

If you have to buy all your flowers you might find it difficult to make an arrangement with a wide range of related colours. In this case buy flowers in the two or three colours around which you wish to create the harmony and then use other accessories to increase the colour range and provide the other nuances, the tints, tones and shades.

It goes without saying by now, I hope, that some of these could be leaves, fruits and vegetables. The choice and inclusion of these will have to depend very much on the style and character of the arrangement.

Candles are a great help to the colour-conscious flower arranger and it is well worth while collecting and keeping a stock of these. I suggest that they are used for

Left
Making an arrangement this is a little like painting picture, one builds it up s introducing light and sha well as colour. Stems are in a bowl fitted in the lam stand. The heavy artichok anchored first.

Right
A colour harmony based some leaf colours. The candles help to bring mo the sap green also found variegated kale. The beec preserved, the maple keys dried. The two flower-like items are the calyces of *Cobea scandens*, an annua climbing plant.

Far right and below
See following page

124

their colour value alone, but naturally if you wish to light them that is up to you.

If you are making a table setting then you can call in many more aids. Glass and linen as well as candles and fruit can contribute to the colour harmony of the flowers. Even a base on which the arrangement stands can help. Cover or colour it if necessary. Patterned china is often a help in creating colour harmonies, especially simple ones. I have in mind, for example, a few bright orange flowers in a white container which carries matching bands of the flower colour.

As I said earlier, the stem holders such as Oasis make it possible for us to use a plate as a container. If you have one with a patterned or coloured edge, you have a good and useful foundation on which to create a colour scheme. Even if you cannot exactly match the china colour you are almost certain to be able to find either complementary or analogous colours which will set you on your way. Do not overlook the fact that some leaves and other foliage might be more useful from the colour point of view if they are arranged with their undersides uppermost.

Sometimes the colour of the glaze of the interior of a low dish can enhance the floral colour. When flowers are set to one side of such a container and arranged on a pinholder or a block of Oasis, the interior of the vessel is often much more in evidence than the outer surface. This is sometimes worth taking into account when you go to buy or gather your flowers. In the same way, the means you employ to conceal the stem holder can contribute to the colour harmony. Stones, lumps of raw glass, coral and sea shells, can all add one or more hues to the whole.

Do not hesitate, either, to use whole plants as flowers at a focal point in a flower arrangement. You can always slip its pot inside a plastic bag so that it does not get over-watered. Think how attractive a little cyclamen, a variegated cryptanthus or a *Begonia rex* might look under certain circumstances.

Finally, having described so many different combinations and mentioned various combinations encouraging you to mix together plants and flowers, fresh or dried, vegetables, fruits and berries, wood, shells and other accessories, one word of warning: do not forget that it is possible to over-elaborate and that the individual beauty of many plants is often sufficient, depending on their position and type. You can only experiment, and half the joy of plants and flowers is in the fun you can have trying endless variations and combinations to suit your home.

Previous page far right
Christmas colours – red ar
green – are complementar
and we can make a simpl
attractive arrangement by
using a handful of evergr
with red accessories. How
the yellow in the holly lea
and the silver down on th
senecio prompted the use
silver and gold baubles an
honesty.

Previous page below
An arrangement for a sum
dining table in which ver
blooms are used. Colour
comes from the red plasti
trug, ornamental kale,
aubergines, currant toma
beans, fennel flower, pans
nasturtiums and three sp
chrysanthemums.

All the spectrum colours a represented here in a rich mixture of autumnal flowe foliage, berries and seed h Few of the flowers are one colour. Most have one or n hues which blend them all one harmonic unit.

Index

Acknowledgments

The publishers would like to thank the following individuals and organizations for their kind permission to reproduce the pictures in this book.

A–Z Botanical Collection: 21 above right; 25 above right; 41 above left; 57 above; Agence Top: 6–7; Bernard Alfieri: 14–15 above; 15 below; 18; 47; 50; Julia Clements: 100 centre; Connaissance des Arts (R. Guillemot): 92 above right; W. F. Davidson: 26–27; 51; J. E. Downward: 33 below; 38–39; 40 above; Douglas Fisher Productions: 34; 88–89; A. Huxley: 12 below; 56; 97 above; George Hyde: 16 below; 40–41 below; 41 above right; 43 above;

45 centre; 45 below; Jackson & Perkins: 11; 22 below; Leslie Johns: 1; 4–5; 8–9; 10; 13; 14 below; 20; 21 below; 22 above; 24; 25 left; 27–32; 33 above; 35 above; 35 below; 36; 42; 44 above; 46; 48; 49 above; 49 below; 54; 57 below; 58–87; 90 above; 90 below; 92 above 'eft; 92 below; 94 above; 96; 97 below; 98–99; 100 above; 100 below; 101–103; 105–109; 111–126; Bill McLaughlin: 23; 53; 94 below; 95; NHPA (B. Alfieri): 43 below; W. Schect: 91; Kenneth Scowen: 36–37; 110; Harry Smith Horticultural Photographic Collection: 55; 93; 104; Spectrum Colour Library: 12 above; 15 below right; 16–17 above; 19; 25 below right; W. J. W. Unwin Ltd: 44 below; 45 above.